# Walk Around

## Bf 110G

### By Ron Mackay

**Color by Don Greer and Andrew Probert**

Illustrated by Ernesto Cumpian and Andrew Probert

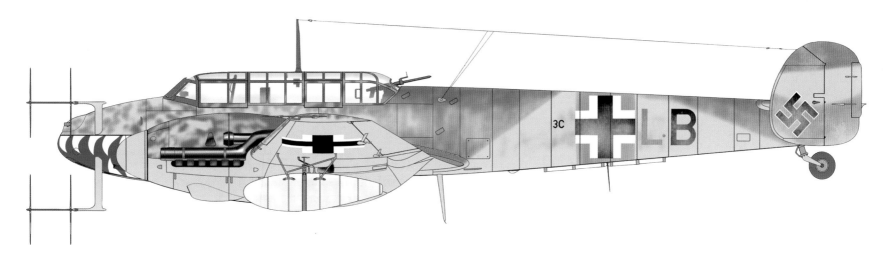

Walk Around Number 24

squadron/signal publications

# Introduction

The Messerschmitt **Bf 110** was one of four major German Air Force (Luftwaffe) or British Royal Air Force (RAF) designs whose ultimate night fighter role was scarcely envisaged during its creation and service introduction. (The other three aircraft were the Junkers Ju 88, the Bristol Beaufighter, and the de Havilland Mosquito.) Survivors of the RAF Bomber Command's Night Offensive surely testify to the Bf 110's efficient performance in night fighter duties during World War II. This testimony cannot be supported by the thousands of RAF crewmen who did not survive their aircrafts' demise at the hands of the Messerschmitt 'twin.' Despite the Bf 110's prominent role in the night skies over Europe, it must not be forgotten that this aircraft also provided sound ground attack service between 1941 and 1943. Additionally, the Bf 110G-2 day fighter was used with reasonable success in Home Defense duties against the B-17s and B-24s of the 8th and 15th United States Army Air Forces (USAAF).

The Bf 110 was developed as a *Zerstörer* (Destroyer) or strategic fighter during the 1930s. The strategic fighter possessed long range for escorting bomber formations deep into enemy territory and an ability to destroy enemy bomber formations threatening friendly territory. This aircraft was also suitable for ground attack missions in support of German troops. The Bf 110V1 prototype first flew on 12 May 1936; however, problems with the aircraft's handling and its original Daimler Benz DB 600A engines resulted in the slightly modified Bf 110V2 being delivered that October. The Luftwaffe chose Messerschmitt's aircraft over the Focke-Wulf Fw 57 and the Henschel Hs 124 in 1937. Only small numbers of the early Bf 110A and Bf 110B variants were built before the Bf 110C – the first major production version – entered operational service in January of 1939.

The contemporary photography in this book has relied solely on the single existing intact Bf 110, which is located at the RAF Museum at Hendon, North London. It is fortunate that the vast bulk of this aircraft's internal and external equipment is original. Over a two-year period, I have been extremely dependent upon the good will and expertise of the volunteers responsible for looking after the five Luftwaffe aircraft currently displayed at the RAF Museum. Peter Nash (Team Leader) and Mike Shilton in particular have furnished me with comprehensive details of the Bf 110's technical and historic background. To this duo, as well as the other individuals within the Volunteer Team, I express my unconditional gratitude.

## Acknowledgements

My thanks are expressed towards several persons who supplied valuable information in respect of the Bf 110. Much of the photography was taken by my regular 'expert' with the camera, Colin Francis. Thanks are also due to the RAF Museum's Andrew Simpson for his courtesy while conducting me on the official photography session. I have made prior reference in the Introduction section to the RAF Museum Volunteer Team, without whose individual and corporate assistance this project would have been much more protracted, if not difficult. I make no apologies for repeating my everlasting thanks!

PHOTO CREDITS
Karl-Fritz Schroeder
Ernie McDowell
Bruce Robertson
Simon Parry

(Front Cover) *Major* Heinz-Wolfgang Schnaufer's Bf 110G-4 (G9+BA) flies away from the RAF Halifax he has successfully attacked on 21 February 1945, when he shot down seven Halifaxes and Lancasters. This was his greatest single success within a final total of 121 'kills' during World War II. At this time, Schnaufer was *Kommodore* (Commander) of NJG (*Nachtjagdgeschwader*; Night Fighter Wing) 4. Although the unit was equipped with Junkers Ju 88s, Schnaufer brought his Bf 110G-4 from his former unit (IV/NJG 1). He preferred to fly the Bf 110G over the heavier Ju 88.

ISBN 0-89747-420-1

If you have any photographs of aircraft, armor, soldiers or ships of any nation, particularly wartime snapshots, why not share them with us and help make Squadron/Signal's books all the more interesting and complete in the future. Any photograph sent to us will be copied and the original returned. The donor will be fully credited for any photos used. Please send them to:

**Squadron/Signal Publications, Inc.**
**1115 Crowley Drive**
**Carrollton, TX 75011-5010**

Если у вас есть фотографии самолётов, вооружения, солдат или кораблей любой страны, особенно, снимки времён войны, поделитесь с нами и помогите сделать новые книги издательства Эскадрон/Сигнал ещё интереснее. Мы переснимем ваши фотографии и вернём оригиналы. Имена приславших снимки будут сопровождать все опубликованные фотографии. Пожалуйста, присылайте фотографии по адресу:

**Squadron/Signal Publications, Inc.**
**1115 Crowley Drive**
**Carrollton, TX 75011-5010**

軍用機、装甲車両、兵士、軍艦などの写真を所持しておられる方はいらっしゃいませんか？どの国のものでも結構です。作戦中に撮影されたものが特に良いのです。Squadron/Signal社の出版する刊行物において、このような写真は内容を一層充実し、興味深くすることができます。当方にお送り頂いた写真は、複写の後お返しいたします。出版物中に写真を使用した場合は、必ず提供者のお名前を明記させて頂きます。お写真は下記にご送付ください。

**Squadron/Signal Publications, Inc.**
**1115 Crowley Drive**
**Carrollton, TX 75011-5010**

(Previous Page) This Bf 110G-4, 3C+LB, was assigned to *Stab* (Headquarters), I *Gruppe* (Group)/NJG (*Nachtjagdgeschwader*; Night Fighter Wing) 4 at Florennes, France during the summer of 1944. The day fighter camouflage of RLM74 Gray Green (FS34086) and RLM75 Gray Violet (FS36122) has been sprayed over the aircraft's uppersurfaces; the undersurfaces remained in RLM76 Light Gray (FS36473). The Bf 110G-4 is equipped with the SN-2b radar antenna on the nose. The night fighter's sharkmouth was from the aircraft's previous assignment with II/ZG (*Zerstörergeschwader*; Destroyer Wing) 76, the *Haifischgruppe* (Shark Group).

(Back Cover) NJG 200 operated at night with visual *Helle Nachtjagd* (Illuminated Night Fighter) tactics on the Russian Front. This Bf 110G-2 (8V+EM) was assigned to the Wing's 4. *Staffel* (Squadron) when NJG 200 was based at Odessa in the Crimea.

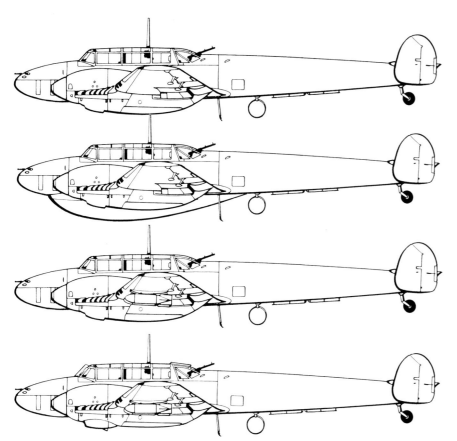

## Bf 110C

The Bf 110C was the first major production variant of Messerschmitt's *Zerstörer* (Destroyer). Powered by two 1050 HP Daimler-Benz DB 601A engines, the Bf 110C entered service in early 1939. This variant was employed for bomber escort, fighter-bomber, and reconnaissance missions. The Bf 110C was also the Luftwaffe's first night fighter aircraft, first seeing action in this role in 1940.

## Bf 110D

The Bf 110D was designed to offer increased range over the earlier Bf 110C. Originally fitted with a 317 gallon (1200 L) underbelly tank, the aircraft was redesigned to carry two 238 gallon (900 L) drop tanks under the wings. The heavy fighter first saw combat during the Battle of Britain during the summer of 1940. The Bf 110D's long range allowed it to fly long-range maritime escort missions.

## Bf 110E

The Bf 110E was designed for the fighter-bomber role and was equipped with bomb racks under the fuselage and wings capable of carrying up to 2667 lbs (1200 KG) of ordnance. Two DB 601N engines supplied power for the Bf 110E. This variant was introduced in the late spring of 1941 and saw service over the Eastern Front, the Mediterranean, and North Africa.

## Bf 110F

The Bf 110F featured redesigned engine nacelles to accept the two 1350 HP DB 601F engines powering this variant. Entering service in early 1942, the Bf 110F was primarily built as a fighter-bomber, although examples were built for the destroyer, reconnaissance, and night fighter roles. This model was intended to be the final Bf 110 variant; however, problems with the Me 210 resulted in the Bf 110F being refined into the Bf 110G.

The only complete Bf 110 known to exist is displayed in the Battle of Britain Hall of the Royal Air Force (RAF) Museum at Hendon, England. This Bf 110G-4 (D5+RL, *Werke Nummer*/Factory Number 730301) was captured by British forces at Grove, Denmark in May of 1945. Three months later, this aircraft was flown to the Royal Aircraft Establishment (RAE) Test Center at Farnborough, England. The Bf 110G-4 was refurbished for five years at RAF St. Athan, Wales before delivery to the RAF Museum in 1978.

This Bf 110G-4 is equipped with the *Lichtenstein* SN-2b air intercept radar, formally designated FuG (*Funk Geräte*/Radio Device) 220 by the Luftwaffe. The Germans called the massive radar antennas *Hirschgeweih* (Stag's Antlers). The drag caused by these antennas reduced the Bf 110G-4's top speed by approximately 25 MPH (40 KMH).

Four angled frames extending from the nose cone supported twin SN-2b antennas, which were positioned vertically on horizontal extension rods. The antennas and extension rods were rounded to reduce drag. The lower right set of antennas had been twisted out of its normal alignment. White stripes painted on the lower antennas increased their visibility on the ground.

A blanking plate has been placed inside the Bf 110G-4's nose bulge air intake. Air passed through the intake to cool the two 30mm (1.2 inches) Rheinmetall Mk 108 cannons which flank the intake. The staggered installation of these weapons resulted in the starboard 30mm cannon muzzle protruding from the aircraft.

The gun bay access panel was removed to allow access to the Bf 110G-4's two 30mm Mk 108 cannons and their ammunition boxes. This arrangement allowed faster access to the ammunition boxes for servicing or reloading. The starboard weapon is staggered forward to provide clearance for the ammunition boxes. Each cannon was supplied with 135 rounds of ammunition.

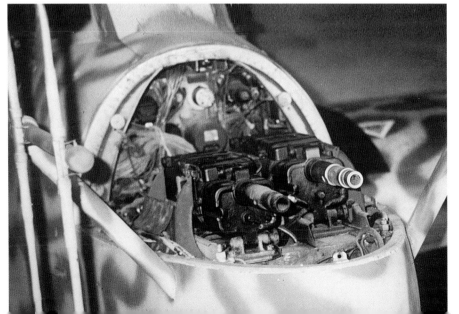

Two 30mm (1.2 inch) Rheinmetall Mk 108 cannons were mounted in the Bf 110G's nose, replacing the four 7.92mm (0.3 inch) MG17 machine guns of earlier Bf 110s. The Mk 108 cannon measured 45 inches (114.3 cm) in length – including 23 inches (58.4 cm) for the barrel – and weighed 135 pounds (61 kg). The SN-2b radar antenna supports flanking the gun bay were angled out from the bay.

5

# Bf 110G Radar Antennas

## FuG 202

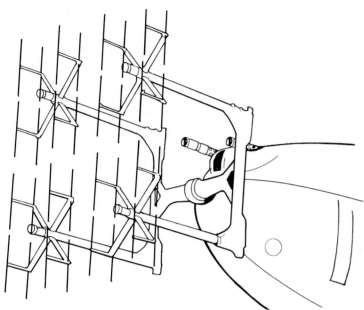

## FuG 220 (SN-2d)

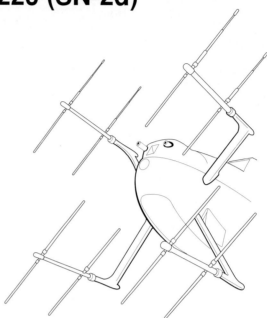

## FuG 212 and SN-2

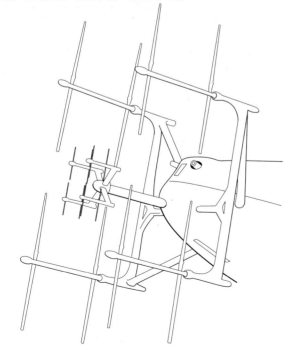

## FuG 218

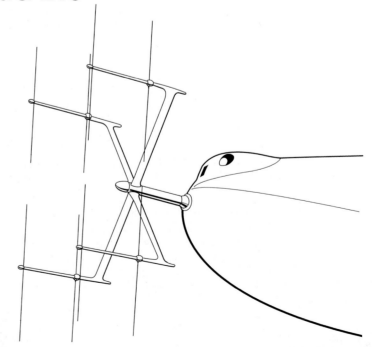

Ammunition for the port 30mm Mk 108 cannon was fed into the weapon through a chute mounted to the left of the cannon's breech. Space for a MG ESK2000 gun camera – not fitted to this aircraft – was provided under the cannon barrels. This camera was used to record gun firing results and was normally placed behind the circular cover under the port 30mm cannon's muzzle.

The two Mk 108 cannon were charged and triggered by compressed air fed to the weapons by electro-pneumatic valves. The compressed air bottle unit servicing the guns was accessed on the port side of the Bf 110G-4's nose. The air bottle was pressurized at 150 atü (*Atmosphärenüberdruck*; atmospheric over pressure).

The Bf 110G-4's upper nose fairing was removable to allow maintenance crews access to the weapons and gun camera. The two 30mm Mk 108 cannons fired through circular apertures in the nose fairing's front section. The rectangular inlet fed cooling air into the gun bay. Overheated weapons could lead to a jamming or gun bay explosion.

A red and white segmented circle surrounds a second compressed air bottle access point on the Bf 110G-4's port nose area. The black lettering around the circle reads: *Preßluft f. Fahrw Notbetatigung 150 atü* (Compressed air for emergency operation of landing gear 150 atmospheres). Compressed air was also used to lower the landing gear if the main gear extension system was out of operation.

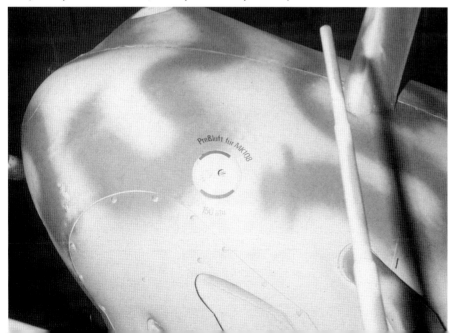

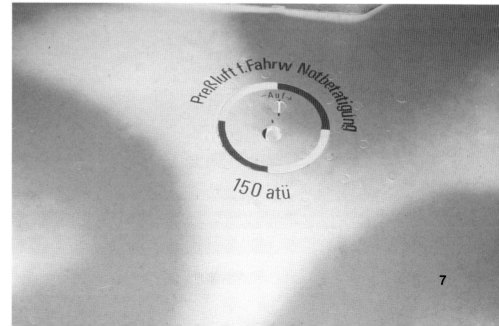

7

The Bf 110G-4 mounted two 20mm (0.8 inch) Mauser MG151/20 cannons in the lower fuselage and fired through oval ports. The detachable weapons servicing panel extended back to the front of the ventral pack. The port 20mm cannon had 300 rounds of ammunition, while the starboard weapon had 350 rounds due to increased room for the latter gun's ammunition box.

Removing the servicing panel reveals the 20mm cannons' blast tubes connecting the weapons to the firing ports. Both tubes are supported on center and rear-mounted brackets. The spent shell case ejection chutes for the two nose-mounted 30mm Mk 108 cannons are fitted just behind the main radar antenna supports.

A shallow scoop was located around the center of the 20mm MG151/20 cannon service panel. This scoop permitted excess fumes and gas from the weapons' operation to escape from the aircraft, eliminating the danger of an explosion. The MG151/20 could fire 780 rounds per minute with a muzzle velocity of 2656 feet (810 m) per second.

A rectangular sheet metal guard is fitted above the starboard upper nose shell ejector chute. This guard deflected 30mm shell casings away from the starboard engine. No similar fitting was installed for the port cannon shell ejector chute, since there was no danger of port engine nacelle damage from ejected shell casings.

The 20mm MG 151/20 cannon were mounted on circular support frames in the Bf 110G-4's lower fuselage. The weapon had an overall length of 69.5 inches (176.5 cm), including a barrel length of 43.5 inches (110.5 cm). The barrel weighed 22.9 pounds (10.3 kg). Spent cannon shells were ejected from the aircraft through chutes located directly behind the support frames. The cannon muzzles extended forward into their blast tubes.

9

The Bf 110G-4 main cockpit canopy consists of nine vertical frames – including seven frames aft of the cockpit – with twin horizontal strips located towards the canopy top edges. Plexiglas panels lie flush with the canopy frames. The main cockpit canopy remained unchanged from the early Bf 110B aircraft through the G model.

The Bf 110G-4's Plexiglas windshield is solidly framed along its top and sides. A 3.5 inch (90MM) thick piece of armored glass is secured over the front of the windshield by threaded bolts at the top and bottom of the frame. The tube running along the bottom frame supplied fuel used to clean the windshield in flight.

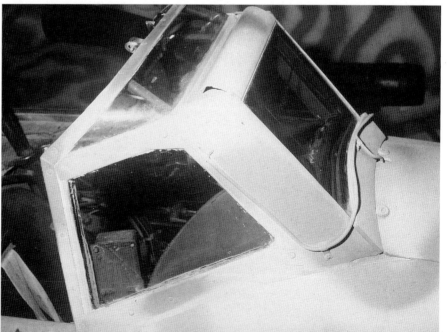

The Bf 110G-4 pilot's canopy consisted of three Plexiglas panels. The top panel was attached to the main cockpit frame and dropped down and forward with the front panel edge fitting to the top of the windshield. The two side canopy panels closed upwards to fit with the top panel.

The Bf 110G-4's two side pilot's canopy panels are hinged along the top of the fuselage to close upward. The forward canopy panel sections can be slid back to allow fresh air inside, along with communications between the pilot and ground crewmen. The side and top canopy panels can only be secured in position from inside the cockpit.

The upper main canopy panel swung on two flexible hinges, which retained this panel in the open position while the Bf 110G-4 was on the ground. A D/F (Direction Finding) loop antenna is mounted immediately aft of the canopy frame. The pilot adjusted the D/F loop to receive radio signals from ground stations. These signals enabled the pilot to adjust or maintain his course.

The Bf 110G-4's control column slants forward from under the vertically aligned handgrip. A leather cover protects the stick's base where it connects with the control cables. The round button on top of the handgrip is an alternative weapons firing button *(Knopf)*. This button operates alternative weapons, such as *schräge Musik* (jazz music) upward firing guns. The raised spoon-shaped item *(Löffel)* covers this button when lowered.

The pilot's seat is a simple one-piece item, which was hollowed out in the base to accommodate the pilot's seat-mounted parachute pack. The seat harness consists of two lap straps attached to the seat sides and two shoulder straps extending down from the top center of the seat. The seat is similar to the ones used in the single engine Bf 109B through Bf 109E fighters.

The Bf 110G-4's windshield frame includes two curved handgrips placed at the top. The pilot used these grips for assistance in entering and leaving the cockpit. The red knob at the top of the windshield frame connected to the canopy locking lever, which secured the upper canopy panel in place. World War II German cockpit interiors were generally painted RLM66 Black Gray (FS36081) after 1941/1942.

The Bf 110G-4's throttle quadrant is mounted on the port side of the cockpit, beside the front edge of the pilot's seat. Slots outside of the throttle levers contained the fuel system priming levers on earlier Bf 110 variants; however, these levers were deleted on the Bf 110G. The seat height adjustment handle protrudes immediately beside the seat.

The two throttle levers – one for each of the Bf 110G-4's DB 605D-1 engines – at the front of the quadrant have Yellow knobs on top. The levers with red knobs behind the throttle are fuel cock controls used to regulate the amount of fuel going to the engines. Magneto switches for starting the engines are placed immediately in front of the throttle quadrant.

The elevator fore-and-aft trim wheel – missing its winding handle – is fitted to the port cockpit wall. The pilot turned this wheel to adjust the trim tab mounted at the trailing edge of the elevator. The Black landing flap position indicator is placed directly above the fuel cock levers.

Magneto switches were mounted on the console top directly ahead of the throttle levers. The two black knurled-surface wheels in front of the console control the landing gear and flap emergency actuation valves. The small console above and to port of these wheels contains the propeller automatic pitch control levers.

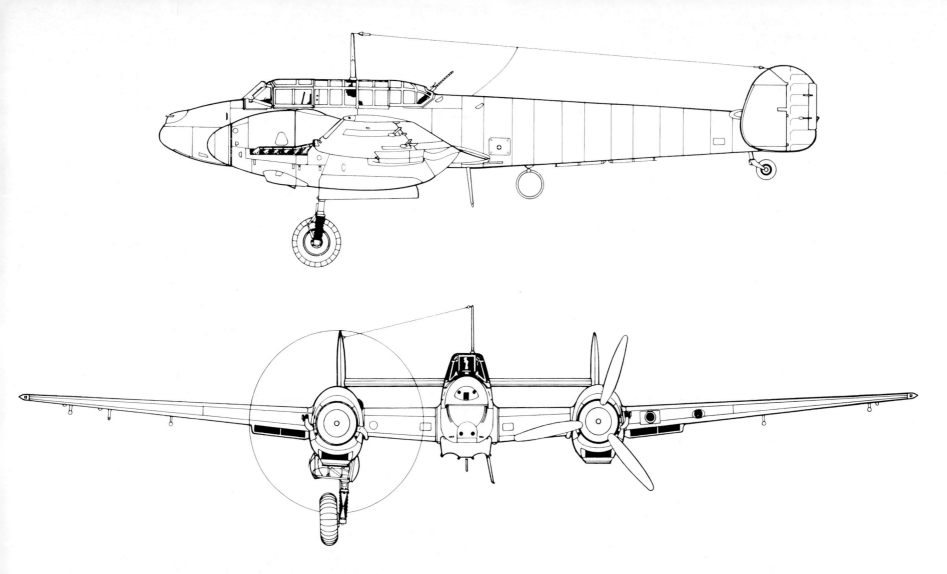

# Messerschmitt Bf 110G-2 Specifications

| | | |
|---|---|---|
| Wingspan | 53 feet 3.75 inches (16.3 M) | |
| Overall Length | 39 feet 7.25 inches (12.1 M) | |
| Height | 13 feet 8.5 inches (4.2 M) | |
| Empty Weight | 11,220 pounds (24,684 KG) | |
| Maximum Weight | 21,800 pounds (47,960 KG) | |
| Powerplants | Two 1475 HP Daimler Benz DB 605B-1, 12-cylinder, inline, liquid-cooled engines | |

**Armament** Two nose-mounted 30MM Mk 108 cannon with 135 rounds per gun (RPG), two lower fuselage-mounted 20MM MG151/20 cannon with 300 RPG (Port) and 350 RPG (Starboard); one rear cockpit 7.92MM MG81Z twin-barreled machine gun with 800 RPG.

**Maximum Speed** 342 MPH (551 KMH) at 22,900 feet (6984.5 M)

**Service Ceiling** 26,250 feet (8006 M)

**Maximum Range** 1305 miles (2101 KM) with two 78 gallon (300 L) drop tanks

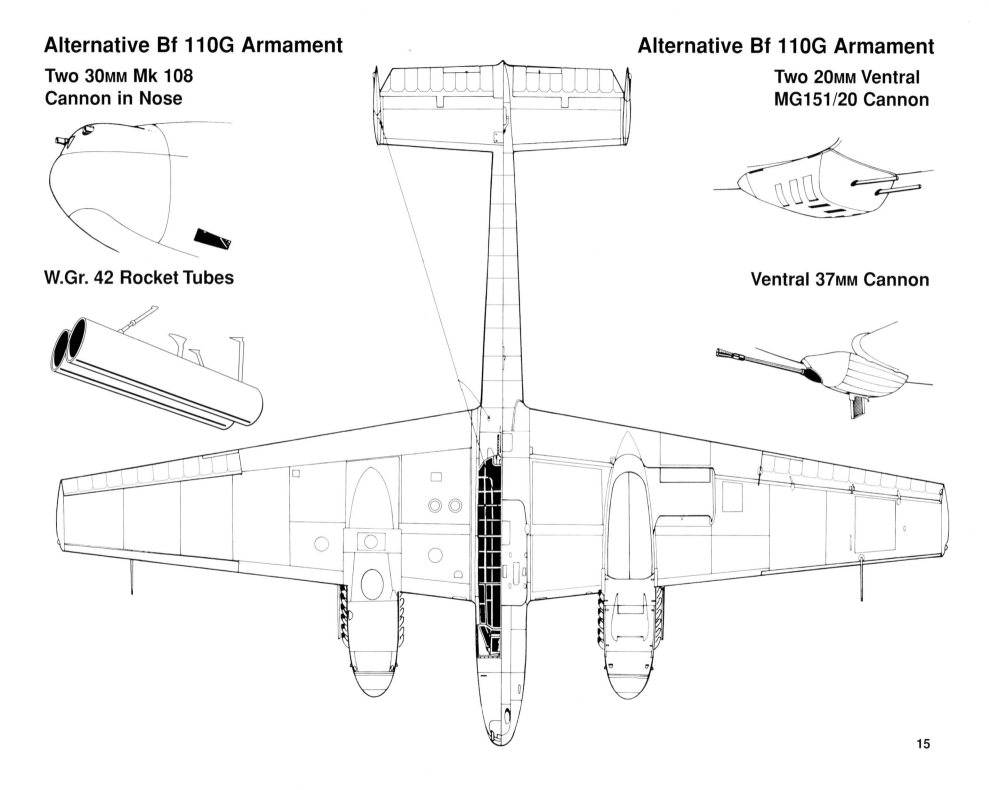

# Alternative Bf 110G Armament

## Two 30ᴍᴍ Mk 108 Cannon in Nose

## W.Gr. 42 Rocket Tubes

# Alternative Bf 110G Armament

## Two 20ᴍᴍ Ventral MG151/20 Cannon

## Ventral 37ᴍᴍ Cannon

The base for the Bf 110G-4's Revi (*Reflexvisier*; Reflector Sight) C/12D reflector gunsight is placed atop the main instrument panel coaming. The artificial horizon dial is installed in the panel's left center portion. A group of four dials in line with the top of the control column monitor engine revolutions and boost. Fuel contents, coolant and coolant radiator monitoring dials are located at the instrument panel's bottom.

The foot-shaped rudder pedal frame is formed from aluminum alloy, with integral heel plates. Foot retaining straps are mounted at the front end of the frame. This was the standard rudder pedal fitted to most German aircraft during World War II. The rudder pedals are connected to the Bf 110's two rudders by cables.

The rudder trim lever with a brown knob is mounted on top of the console. A section of yellow covered electrical wiring runs through the console beside the trim lever. Two black engine start-up handles are placed left of the trim lever. Behind the start-up handles are the silver fuel system selection switches. The aircraft lighting dimmer switch is directly ahead of the rudder trim lever. The control stick has been pulled to starboard.

The black plastic grip of the Bf 110G-4's control stick features a pebbled finish to improve the pilot's grip. The spoon-shaped *Löffel* – the nose armament firing lever – is lowered over the weapons button, preventing the accidental use of the aircraft's alternate weapons.

The crash pylon immediately behind the pilot's seat extends down to the cockpit floor, where the pylon's outer vertical posts are anchored. The pylon bore all likely loads upon the cockpit in the event the aircraft overturned. Bracing stays for the top hinged canopy panel are linked to channels mounted between the top of the crash pylon and the front of the main canopy frame. The pilot's shoulder harness feeds through the seat back slot.

17

Immediately behind the opened pilot's top canopy section are the D/F (Direction Finder) loop antenna and the radio mast. The D/F loop is centrally positioned on top of the canopy, while the mast is offset to port. The radar operator's instruments are placed in the front section of the aft cockpit, immediately behind the radio mast.

The radio mast on the Bf 110G-4 displayed at Hendon, England is a substitute item for the original fitting, which was lost at some stage of the aircraft's post-war career. The mast normally supports twin antenna wires extending back to the top of the vertical fins. Screws secure the mast's base to the canopy frame.

The Bf 110G-4's rear canopy section takes up approximately half of the overall canopy length. This canopy can be jettisoned in flight by releasing four retention bolts. The 7.92ᴍᴍ MG81Z *Zwilling* (Twin) machine gun is mounted at the aft end of the rear canopy.

# DF Loop Antenna and Antenna Mast

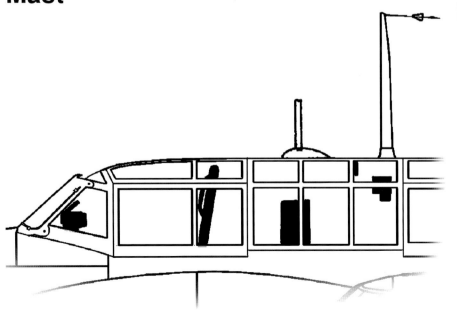

The Bf 110G-4's Direction Finding (D/F) loop antenna is mounted on a teardrop base. Earlier Bf 110 models fitted this loop under the fuselage, just ahead of the instrument ('blind') landing system antennas. The D/F antenna received continuous wave radio signals broadcast by ground stations. The pilot used this information to either maintain or adjust his course.

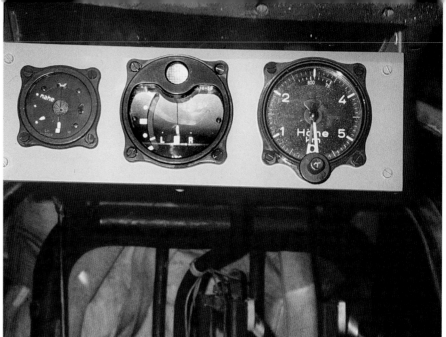

The radar operator's repeater instrument panel is mounted in the rear cockpit's roof. The instruments on this panel are (L-R): a blind-landing receiver indicator, a blind-landing direction dial, and an altimeter. These instruments allowed the radar operator to assist the pilot in 'blind' (instrument only) landings at night or in bad weather.

The marker beacon receiver set is attached to the top left of the Bf 110G-4's rear canopy frame. The repeater instrument panel is placed at the top of the station, while radar controls are located below. Color traces of the original RLM66 Black Gray interior paint appear on the edge of the upper left canopy frame.

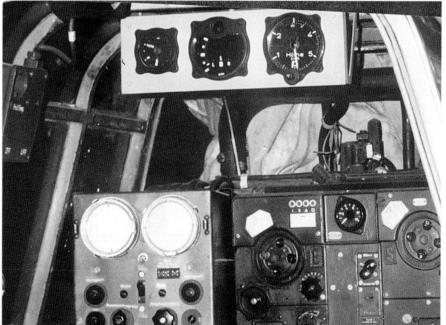

The *Lichtenstein* SN-2b radar equipment is mounted at the upper left portion of the radar operator's station, located immediately behind the pilot's position. The center and lower rows of instrument boxes are the radio and D/F equipment. Bundles of Yellow electrical wiring run along the starboard cockpit wall.

The SN-2 radar set at the top left of the rear cockpit station has twin scopes. The radar operator scans these dials for the bearing and the height of a potential target, then passes this information to the pilot. Alongside the SN-2 is the FuG 16Z VHF (Very High Frequency) radio transmitter/receiver set.

Radio equipment is mounted on the center row of the rear cockpit instrument panel. These units are (L-R): the FuG 10 HF (High Frequency) EK (*Empfänger-Kurzwelle*; short-wave receiver), the FuG 10 MF (Medium Frequency) EL (*Empfänger-Langwelle*; long-wave receiver), and the Peil GV direction-finding indicator.

The 20MM MG151/20 cannon ammunition boxes flanked the radar operator's seat. The port box – a metal container with a wooden cover – held 300 rounds of ammunition for this weapon. The Morse Code box and key for radio transmissions is installed directly above the front end of the port ammunition container. Bf 110G-4 radar operators were also trained as radio operators and were required to send and receive coded and uncoded ('in the clear') Morse Code messages.

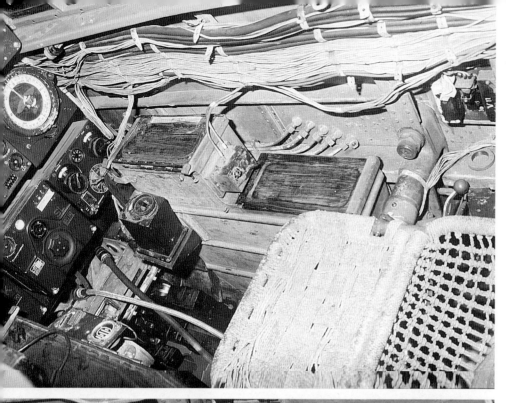

(Above Left) The starboard rear cockpit 20MM ammunition box held 350 rounds – 50 more rounds than the port container due to greater room in the right fuselage for ammunition. The cockpit floor panel was removable to gain access to the MG151/20 cannon. The MG in the weapon's designation stood for *Maschinen Gewehr* (Machine Gun), while 15 represented the originally designed bore diameter in millimeters, and 1 stood for the first model of this gun. The MG151/20 could fire High Explosive (HE), High Explosive Incendiary-Tracer (HEI-T), Armor Piercing Incendiary (API), Armor Piercing High Explosive (APHE), and High Explosive Incendiary (HEI) rounds. Yellow insulation covers for the electrical cables were a regular feature on late-World War II German aircraft. The majority of the Bf 110G-4's controls and wiring were channeled down the starboard side of the fuselage.

(Above) A combined seating unit – removed from the aircraft – served both the Bf 110G-4's radio/radar operator and the rear gunner. The same seating arrangement was used in earlier Bf 110 models. The rear gunner's seat is a simple metal frame with a netting interior, while the radio/radar operator's seat has woven fabric strips. The lower part of the vertical frame contains three spring-clips for holding flares and other items. Flares are fired from a flare pistol for communicating with other aircraft under radio silence conditions and for distress calls.

(Left) The twin-seat unit is installed into the Bf 110G-4's rear cockpit with the waist harness belt clipped to gunner's section's sides. The radio/radar operator's seat belts appear to be missing from this seat unit. The basic nature of the rear cockpit seats provided an uncomfortable ride for either crewman during an extended flight.

# MG81Z *Zwilling* (Twin) Machine Gun

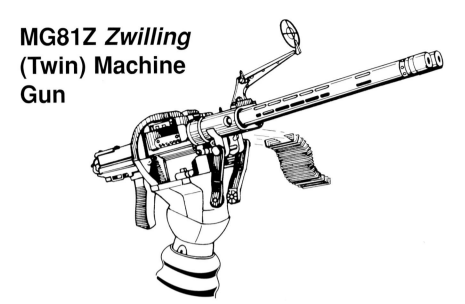

# *schräge Musik* (Slanting, or Jazz Music) Gun Installation (Two 20MM MGFF/M Cannons)

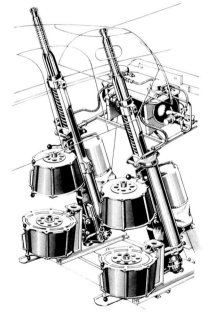

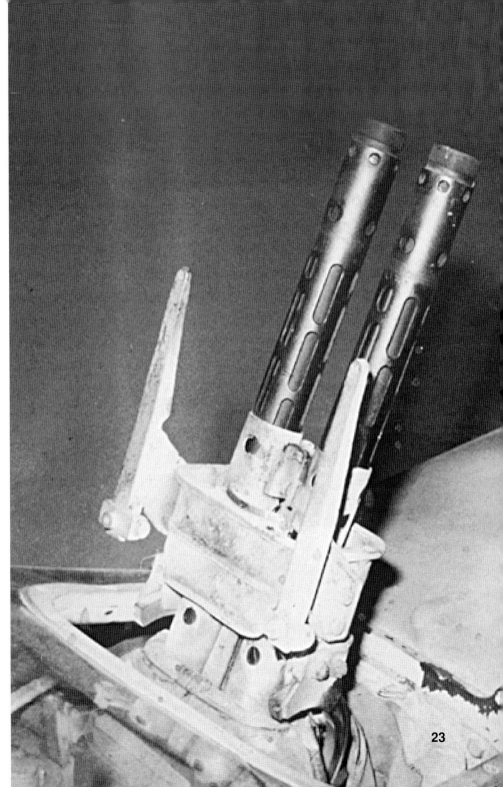

(Right) The Bf 110G's standard rear defensive weapon was the 7.92MM (0.3 inch) Mauser MG81Z *Zwilling* (twin) machine gun. This twin-barreled weapon replaced the single-barrel 7.92MM Rheinmetall MG15 machine gun which equipped earlier Bf 110s. The projections on either side of the support frame are for the gunsights. The MG81Z could fire 1200 to 1500 rounds per minute, with a muzzle velocity of 2500 to 3000 feet (750 to 900 M) per second.

23

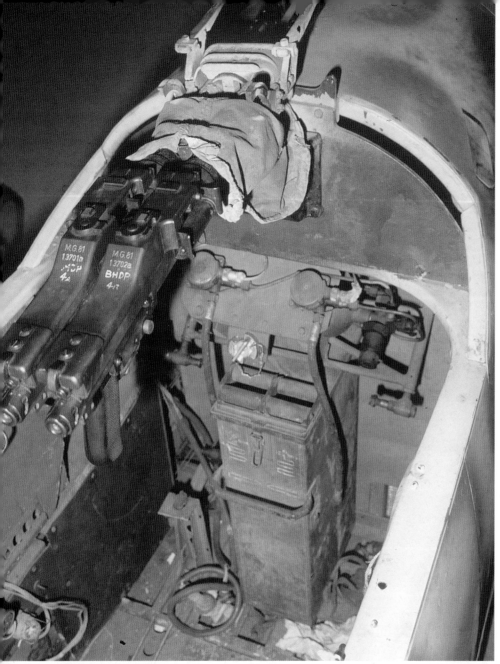

The 7.92MM MG81Z machine gun's twin breeches extend into the Bf 110G-4's rear cockpit. The gunner fired both barrels using the weapon's single pistol-grip. The machine gun's type and serial number are marked on the breech frames' curved portion. Normal overall cockpit color during the time of this aircraft's production was RLM66 Black Gray (FS36081), but this cockpit section appears to have been sprayed RLM02 Gray (FS36165).

The ammunition box for the MG81Z is mounted against the rear cockpit bulkhead, aft of the rear gunner's seat. Rollers on top of this box guide the ammunition into the gun breeches. Stenciled lines on the container indicate the correct method of stacking the ammunition belts inside the box. The MG81Z was supplied with 800 rounds of 7.92MM ammunition.

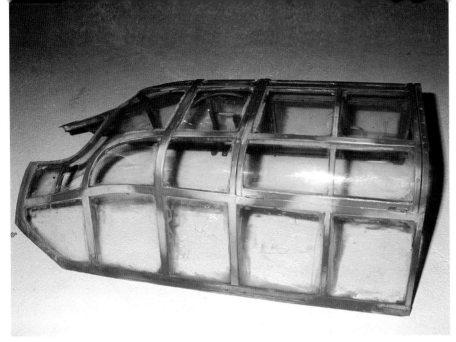

The rear canopy has been detached from the Bf 110G-4. The *Wellenmuster* (wave-pattern) RLM75 Gray Violet (FS36122) camouflage has been extended onto the canopy framework. The Bf 110G's aft gunner fired his gun with the canopy closed; on earlier Bf 110s, the gunner had to open the canopy.

Bf 110G-4 rear cockpit access panel brackets are curved units with slots fitted to the panel ends. Slots are also mounted inside in the brackets' center lengths. Studs attached to the canopy's fixed portion acted as opening and closing guides and prevented the canopy from going beyond a certain point. The access panel could be opened from either inside or outside of the aircraft.

The Bf 110G was the sole variant to have a side-hinged panel for rear cockpit access. This panel is hinged to the top right side of the cockpit frame. Both the rear gunner and the radio/radar operator entered and exited the aircraft through the opening covered by this hinged panel.

The MG81Z machine gun barrels extended through the cut out in the rear of the aft canopy section. The apertures flanking the cutout appear too far aft to be the outlet points for *Schräge musik* (strange, or jazz music) gun barrels. These barrels were normally positioned within the curved frames just ahead of these apertures.

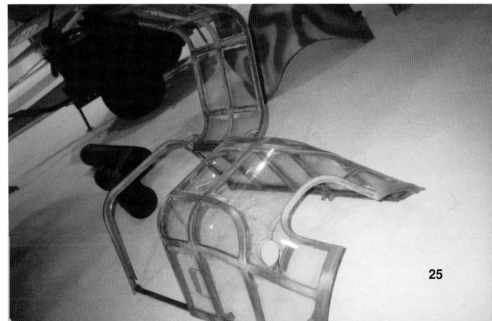

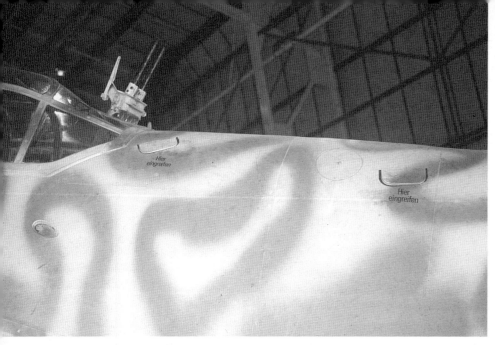

The port side twin handgrip panels are located just behind the Bf 110G-4's rear cockpit frame. The flush-mounted panels are spring laden and push inwards under hand pressure. The flare gun aperture is mounted below the cockpit frame.

The port upper handgrip bears the black stencil *Hier eingreifen* (grasp here). Crewmen used the handgrip to step from the ladder to the wing root, then into the cockpit. The 7.92MM MG81Z twin-barreled machine gun and mount are installed at the rear cockpit's aft end.

The aft handgrip is mounted parallel to the trailing edge wing root on the Bf 110G-4's port side. *Hier eingreifen* (grasp here) is stenciled beside the handgrip as a guide to the crewmen boarding the aircraft. No handgrips are mounted in the Bf 110's starboard fuselage side; crew entry and exit is normally through the port side only.

The Bf 110G-4's retractable crew boarding step was located directly aft of the wing root. The black stenciling beside the step's slot reads *Einsteigleiter Knopf drücken* (press button to lower stepladder). Pressing the button beside the slot lowered the spring-loaded boarding step.

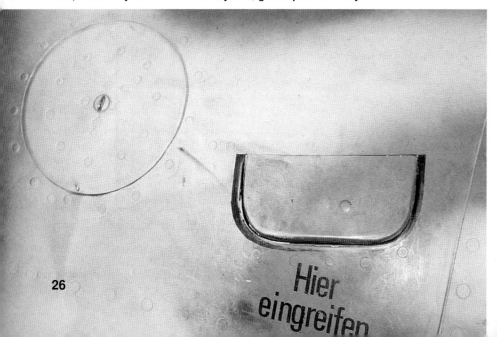

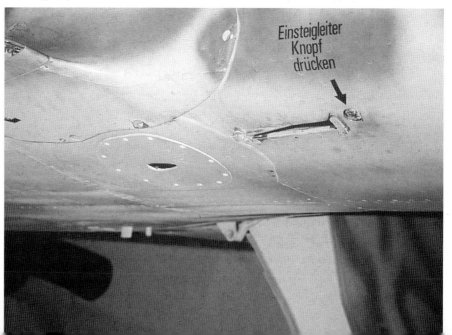

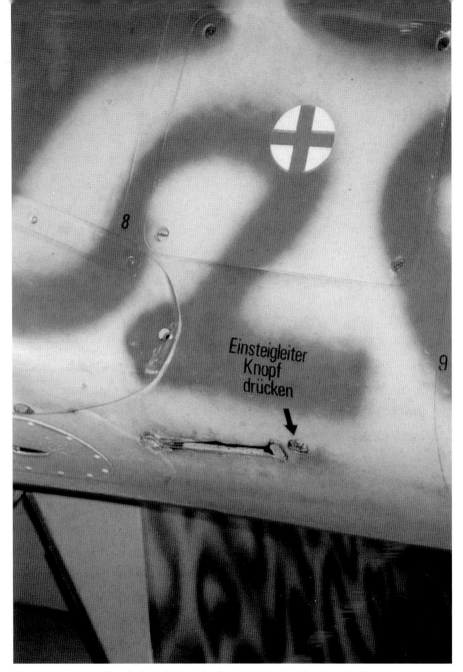

A red cross in a white circle indicates the first-aid kit's location in a fuselage compartment directly behind the port wing root. This detachable panel also provides access to the FuG 10P HF (High Frequency) radio-set and the FuB (*Funk Blind*; Blind Landing Radio) 12F airfield instrument landing receiver set. The aircraft's batteries and a transformer are also located in this compartment.

The Bf 110G-4's crew boarding step has three rungs and is perpendicular to the ground with the aircraft at rest. Once the flight crew was aboard the aircraft, a ground crewman simply pushed the step back up into its well. The step was painted RLM23 Red (FS31140) for high visibility while the Bf 110 was on the ground.

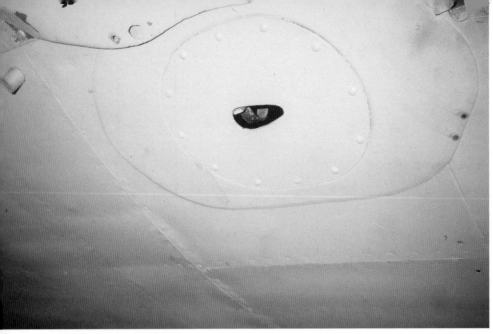

The circular access plate for the ventral antenna is located on the fuselage underside, just ahead of the boarding ladder's position. The undersurface antenna mast is absent from this Bf 110G-4, but this mast would normally protrude aft at a slight angle from the plate's aperture.

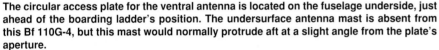

The cover has been removed from the Bf 110G-4's ETC 500 ventral *Waffenwanne* (Weapons Tray). Pairs of sway braces flank the ETC 500's twin central supports. The sway braces serve to retain ordnance firmly in position on the rack, prior to the bombs being released.

The ETC 500 (*Elektrische Trägervorrichung für Cylinderbomben*; Electrically operated carrier for bombs) ventral tray was normally used for carrying ordnance up to an individual weight of 1111 lbs (500 KG). The rack's primary function when fitted to a night fighter would appear to be redundant; however, ground attack was a secondary duty of Luftwaffe night fighter units, especially during the last, desperate months of World War II.

The detached ventral weapons tray cover includes the cutouts for the racks and sway braces. The ETC 500's sway braces fitted through the cover's small fore-and-aft apertures. Two cut-outs located in the cover's center accommodate the 20MM MG151/20 cannon shell-ejector chutes. The cover interior is painted RLM02 Gray.

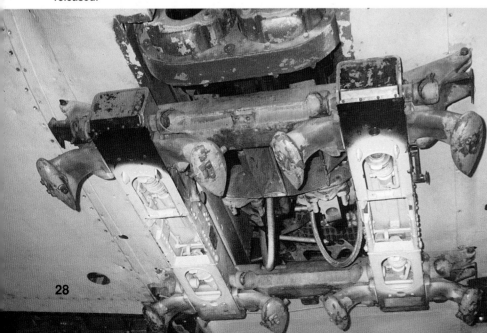

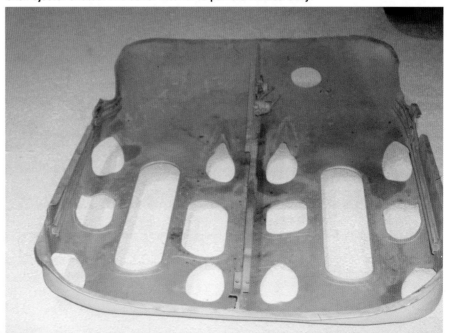

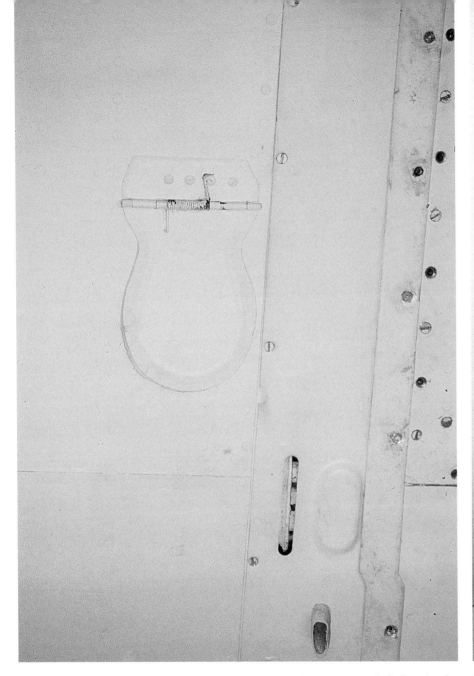

The port lower fuselage aperture located aft of the ventral weapons tray is believed to be the access point for charging the GM-1 nitrous oxide engine boost system. The GM-1 was originally fitted to this Bf 110G-4's rear cockpit. The lower end of the gas filler pipe is covered by a spring loaded door, which is hinged to the front.

The under fuselage spring loaded door is opened to provide access to the nitrous oxide filler pipe, which leads from the aft cockpit. The interior of the door and pipe are painted RLM02 Gray (FS36165), while the aircraft undersurface is painted RLM76 Light Gray (FS36473).

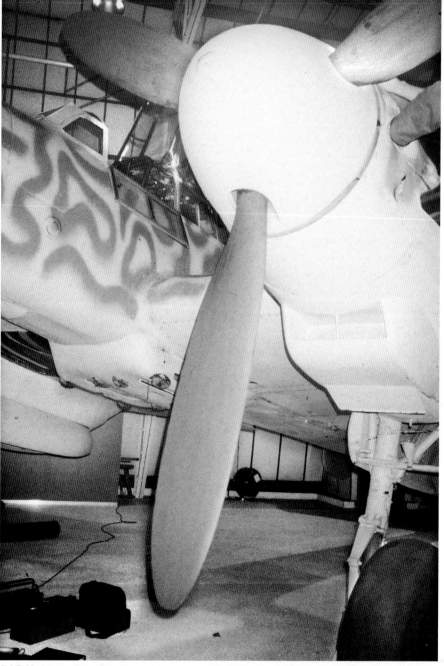

The Bf 110G-4 was equipped with two VDM (*Vereinigte Deutsche Metallwerke*; United German Metalworks) 9-12098A/B three-bladed, constant speed propellers. The pilot could adjust the propeller's pitch to maintain proper engine performance at all speeds and altitudes. The propeller blades were incorrectly painted black when the aircraft was accepted by the RAF Museum in 1978.

RAF Museum aircraft restorers later repainted the Bf 110G-4's propeller blades RLM70 Black Green (FS34050) – the correct German propeller blade color. This propeller is missing the VDM emblem – a triangle with VDM in black – in the center front surfaces of each blade. Each Bf 110G-4 propeller measures 11 feet 2 inches (3.4 м) in diameter.

(Above) Each VDM propeller hub is placed inside a single-piece propeller spinner, which fits flush with the DB605 engine cowling. Maintenance crews could remove the spinner to service the propeller hub. The Bf 110G-4's spinner is painted RLM76 Light Gray (FS36473) to match the surrounding airframe. Other Bf 110s had the spinner painted to match *Staffel* (squadron) colors, airframe uppersurface colors, or with a black and white *Spiralschnauze* (Spiral nose) for recognition purposes. Exhaust flame dampers flank the engine nacelle's sides and the starboard engine's supercharger air duct is mounted on the inboard side of the nacelle. The engine oil cooler intake is mounted beneath the nacelle.

(Above Right) The spinner has been removed to reveal how the VDM 9-12098A/B propeller's three blades are secured into their sockets. Each propeller blade has a threaded base, which screws into the hub. This feature allows maintenance crews to remove and replace individual propeller blades. British restorers painted the propeller hub and spinner back plate in red primer; the Germans actually painted these parts RLM02 Gray (FS36165).

(Right) The propeller spinner has a plate inserted within its forward area, which adds strength to the overall structure. Three cutouts in the sides allow the propeller blades to pass through the spinner. The Bf 110G's propeller spinner was also used on the later Me 210, which was intended to succeed the Bf 110 in the *Zerstörer* (Destroyer) role. The spinner's inner surface is black.

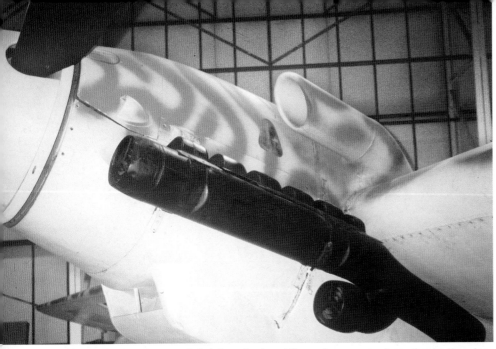

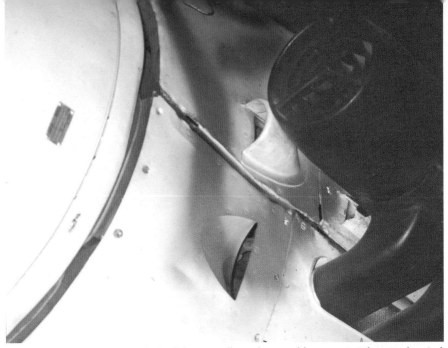

The starboard engine nacelle's inboard exhaust flame damper was ducted under the wing, due to the engine supercharger intake being mounted on the upper cowling. The other three flame dampers are mounted over the wing surfaces. Flame dampers hide engine exhaust flames which would give away the aircraft's presence at night.

The Bf 110G-4's exhaust flame dampers are comprised of two sections. The lower section fits over the exhaust stubs, while the upper section sits in the lower section's 'trough' shape. Circular brackets at the front and rear connect the two flame damper sections.

A recessed air inlet is placed aft of the propeller spinner, with an exposed scoop located above. These scoops direct cooling air onto the engine's exhaust manifolds and spark plugs. The cooling air inlets are placed on both sides of the engine nacelle.

Propeller pitch control indicators and engine performance instruments are installed behind a window in the Bf 110's inboard engine nacelles. These instruments are not repeated in the Bf 110G's cockpit, unlike previous Bf 110 variants. Control levers in the cockpit allow the pilot to adjust the propeller blade pitch required for particular levels of flight performance.

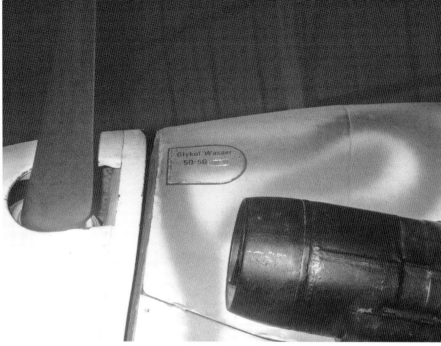

The engine coolant tank filler is located directly aft of the propeller spinner on the port engine cowling. The hinged coolant fill cover is outlined in green and contains the green stenciling *Glykol Wasser 50/50* (glycol water 50/50 mix). Ethylene glycol is a water soluable engine cooling and anti-freeze liquid.

The Bf 110G-4's engine oil cooler is located on the cowling undersurface. The air intake slot – through which air passed to cool the engine oil – is centrally braced for strength. The lower engine cowl and oil cooler cover were built as a single unit. The cowl is secured to the nacelle by snap fasteners placed at the fore and aft ends.

The engine coolant tank filler cover has been opened to reveal the filler cap. The cap is unscrewed for ground crewmen to top off the 50/50 mix of glycol and water used to cool the Bf 110G-4's Daimler Benz DB 605 engines. The door's inner surface was painted red primer by the museum, while the inside of the filler bay is original RLM02 Gray and the cap is natural metal.

33

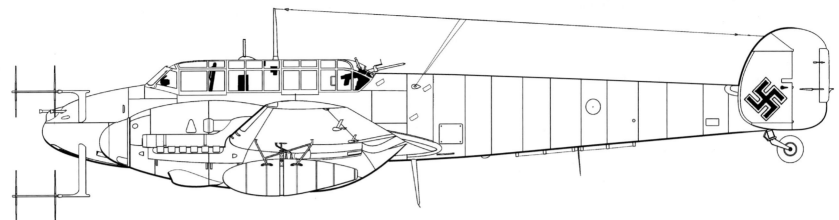

# Messerschmitt Bf 110G-4 Specifications

| | |
|---|---|
| Wingspan | 53 feet 3.75 inches (16.3 M) |
| Overall Length | 42 feet 9.75 inches (13.1 M) |
| Height | 13 feet 8.5 inches (4.2 M) |
| Empty Weight | 11,220 pounds (24,684 KG) |
| Maximum Weight | 21,800 pounds (47,960 KG) |
| Powerplants | Two 1475 HP Daimler Benz DB 605B-1, 12-cylinder, inline, liquid-cooled engines. |
| Armament | Four nose-mounted 7.92MM MG17 machine guns with 1000 rounds per gun (RPG) (Alternately: Two nose-mounted 30MM Mk 108 Cannon with 135 RPG), two lower fuselage-mounted 20MM MG151/20 cannon with 300 RPG (Port) and 350 RPG (Starboard); one rear cockpit 7.92MM MG81Z twin-barreled machine gun with 800 RPG; provision for two 20MM MGFF/M or two 30MM Mk 108 cannon in *schräge Musik* oblique position in aft cockpit. |
| Maximum Speed | 317 MPH (510 KMH) at 22,900 feet (6984.5 M) |
| Service Ceiling | 26,250 feet (8006 M) |
| Maximum Range | 1305 miles (2101 KM) with two 78 gallon (300 L) drop tanks |

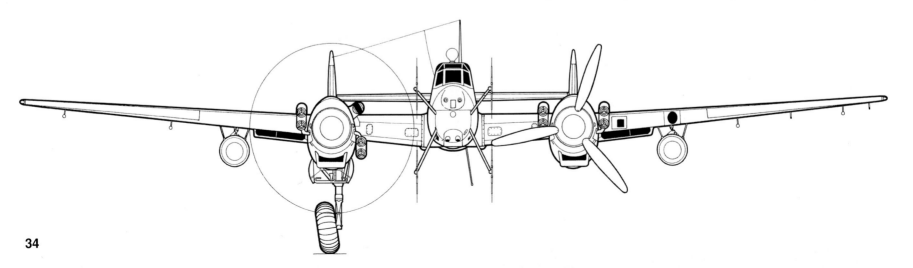

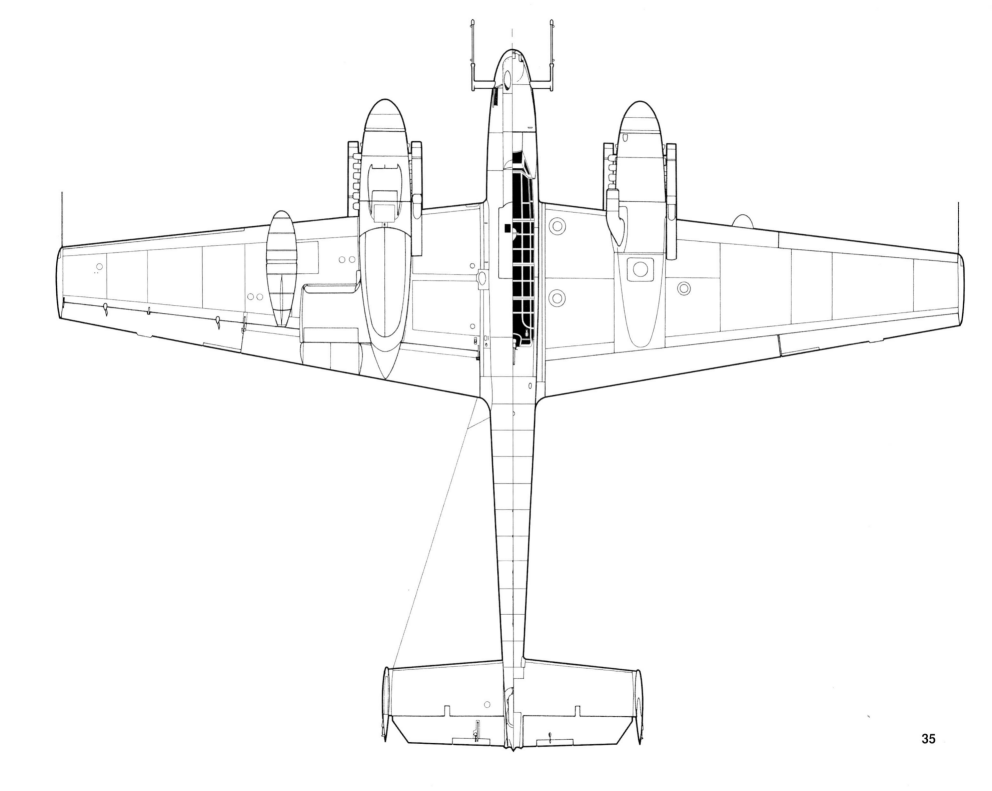

The Bf 110G-4 was powered by the 1475 horsepower (HP) Daimler Benz DB 605B-1 inline, liquid cooled engine. The DB 605 is a 12-cylinder vee-type engine, in which the cylinders are placed in two inclined banks of six cylinders each. This engine block has been restored to its original finish of black with silver spark plugs and plug cables. The super-charger unit is located at the rear of the engine and provided additional air to boost the DB 605B-1's power, particularly at high altitudes.

The starboard engine cowling of the RAF Museum's Bf 110G-4 has been removed to expose the DB 605B-1 engine. This powerplant has not been restored to original condition. The main engine bearer frames run horizontally from the engine block's upper center area to attachment points on the firewall. The DB 605 is an inverted engine, in which the cylinder heads point down. British restorers have incorrectly painted the engine bearer frames red primer.

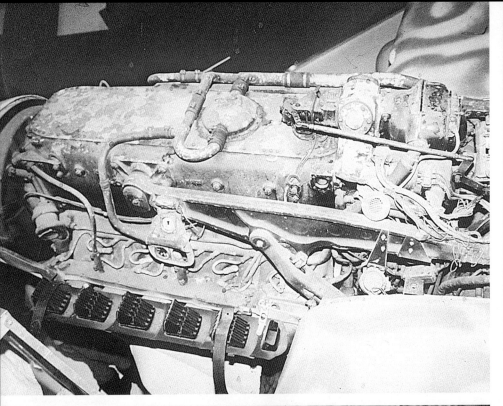

(Above Left) The cowling panels have been removed from the Bf 110G-4's starboard DB 605B-1 engine; however, the propeller spinner remains in place. The lower portion of the exhaust flame damper has been fitted to the six inboard exhaust stacks. The engine bearer frames have been incorrectly painted red primer on this aircraft. A mounting pad is placed where the engine bearer meets the engine block. This pad reduces airframe vibration produced by the engine. Coolant pipes and spark plug cables wind around various areas of the engine block.

(Above) The DB 605B-1 engine's coolant tank is placed aft of the propeller base plate. This circular tank held a mixture of 50 percent ethylene glycol and 50 percent water. The coolant filler cap has been removed. A ring of 0.2 inch (5MM) armor is mounted between the propeller base plate and the engine coolant tank, protecting the tank from damage being inflicted from the front. Spark plug wires connect each cylinder head area on the engine block with the magneto further aft. The propeller pitch indicator and engine performance instruments are placed above the fourth cylinder head.

(Left) Engine instruments are placed in a triangular-shaped unit located on the main engine bearer frame. This unit appears on the inboard sides of both engine nacelles. The upper instrument shows the relative propeller pitch position as selected by the pilot. The other two instruments monitor the engine's performance. When the engine cowling is installed, these instruments are seen through a clear window in the cowling.

(Above) The magneto – mounted above the DB 605B-1 engine's rear section – served as the powerplant's electrical ignition source. The magneto's placement resulted in the bulged aft engine cowling section. Directly below the magneto is the aperture for the supercharger intake. Air was brought through this aperture from the engine cowling scoop.

(Right) The Bf 110G-4's lower engine bearer frame angles down and back from the main frame. Both the main and lower frames are secured to the combination firewall and bulkhead in the engine nacelle. Engine bearer frames are forged from solid steel for the necessary strength to support the powerplant's weight. Black hoses running down the lower engine area are connected with the oil cooler mounted under the engine.

The Bf 110G-4's main landing gear consists of a single leg with an outboard angled main bracing strut. The landing gear, the gear door inner surfaces, and the gear bay are painted RLM76 Light Gray (FS36473). The semi-gloss black wheel sits on the hub drum at a slight outward angle. Tire surfaces normally have a lateral rib pattern, but this appears to be a post-war tire installed by the RAF Museum.

The scissor link mounted on the front of the main landing gear strut prevents the wheel from rotating sideways and prevents over-extension of the oleo (shock absorbing) strut. The RAF Museum's Bf 110G has a steel sleeve covering the chrome oleo; this sleeve prevents the landing gear from sagging. The landing gear is raised on a plinth to reduce stress upon the landing gear and tires.

Main wheel brakes are hydraulically operated with pressure fed from a system, which was independent of the Bf 110G-4's main hydraulic system. Each main wheel was equipped with two brakes. A single brake line ran down the landing gear strut to a fitting on the inner wheel half. A second line ran from this fitting, through the hollow axle, to a second fitting on the outer wheel half.

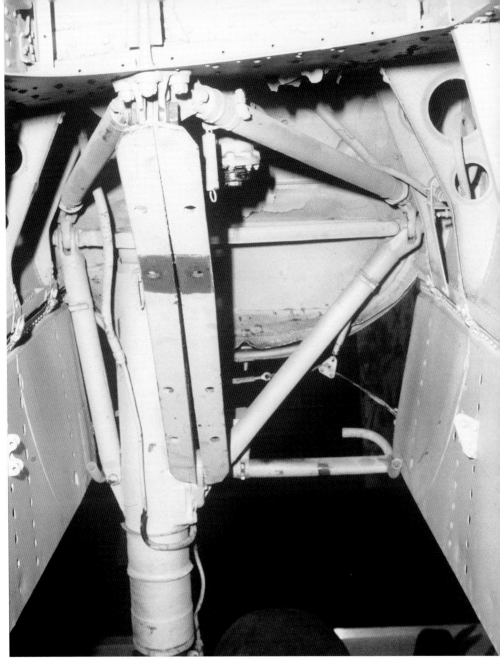

The rearward-retracting main landing gear is mounted in the engine nacelle's front section. Four landing gear support rods are connected from the main gear strut to the cross support on the engine firewall. The brake line runs down the back of the main strut. The RAF Museum staff added two metal braces to the upper main landing gear strut for additional landing gear support.

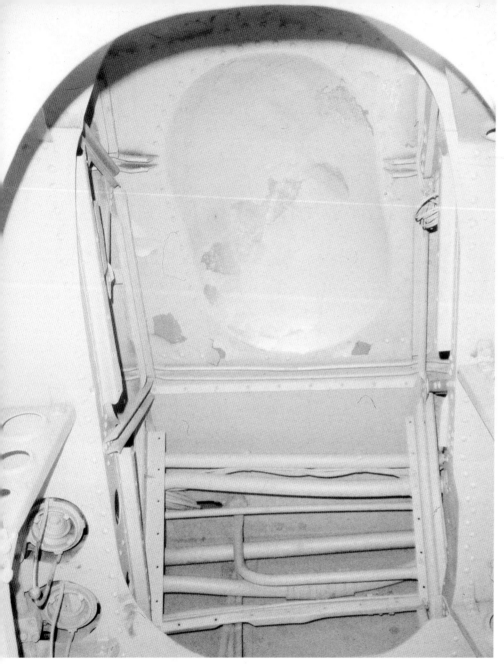

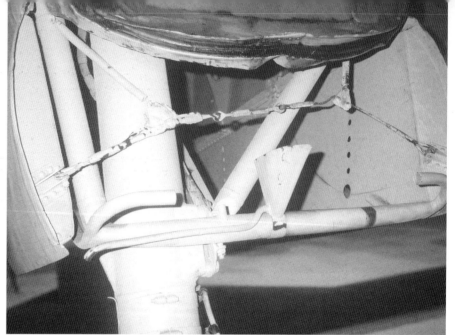

A cable system linking the Bf 110G-4's main landing gear doors passes in front of the upper main gear strut. This cable system allowed the landing gear doors to close during gear retraction and to open the doors when the gear was extended. The Bf 110's landing gear door system was similar to the system used on the de Havilland Mosquito.

# Main Landing Gear Strut and Bay

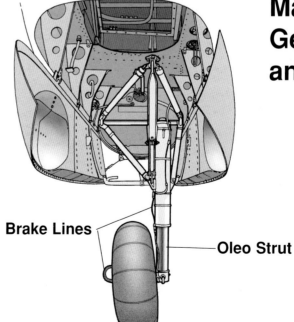

**Brake Lines**

**Oleo Strut**

The upper-rear center section of the main landing gear bay is bulged to accommodate the retracted wheel. Bf 110G-4 wheel bays were normally sprayed RLM76 Light Gray (FS36473); however, late-World War II landing gear bays were also painted RLM02 Gray (FS36165) or left in bare metal.

Each Bf 110G-4's main landing gear door is fastened to the nacelle by four hinges. Each hinge is attached to a structural frame within the engine nacelle for strength. The two gear doors completely enclose the retracted landing gear within the nacelle.

The main landing gear doors are hollowed out at the rear to accommodate the tire when the gear is retracted. The Bf 110G used 36.8 inch (935mm) by 13.6 inch (345mm) main wheel tires. Previous Bf 110 variants were fitted with 34.6 inch (875mm) by 12.6 inch (320mm) tires.

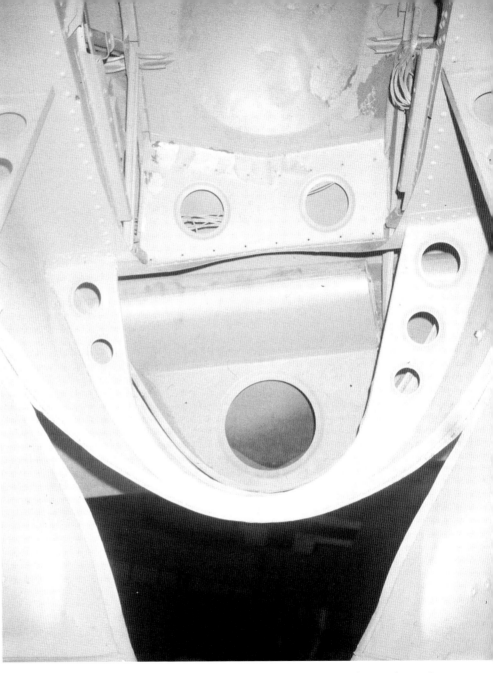

The aft nacelle section provides clearance for the Bf 110G-4's rearward-retracting main landing gear tire. The structural supports inside the nacelle have lightening holes, which reduces the overall structural weight without weakening its basic strength.

The Bf 110G's slotted flaps are single units along the wings' trailing edges, extending from the fuselage to the aileron. The flaps are hydraulically operated and lower to a maximum angle of 55° for landing. A compressed air system is available for emergency flap operation.

The Bf 110G-4's port wing flap has been removed to expose the inner and center fixed flap brackets. The flap was attached to these brackets, which are mounted in the flap well. A fairing attached to the flap filled the gap between the engine nacelle and the flap.

Each wing was attached to the fuselage through four mountings, including this starboard rear wing/fuselage mount. A single circular lug fastened to the wing was slotted into the twin lugs mounted to the fuselage. A large threaded bolt passing through the lugs secured each mounting into position.

The port flap has been reinstalled on the aircraft and includes the nacelle fairing placed right of the yellow primer. This fairing neatly fitted the flap's undersurface to the rear of the main engine nacelle when the flap was up. The upper flap surface was smooth with no interference with the engine nacelle.

Twin antennas located under the port wing's outer section are part of the Bf 110G-4's FuG (*Funk Geräte*; Radio Equipment) 101a radio altimeter equipment. The outboard antenna is the transmitter while the inboard antenna is the receiver. Automatic wing slats were mounted on the wing leading edge.

The FuG 101a radio altimeter antenna is secured to the access panel by small screws and the panel is held in place by four large screws. The access panel is hinged on the inner edge for the transmitter unit and outer edge for the receiver unit. The radio altimeter measured the time radio waves reflected off the ground, indicating the aircraft's altitude.

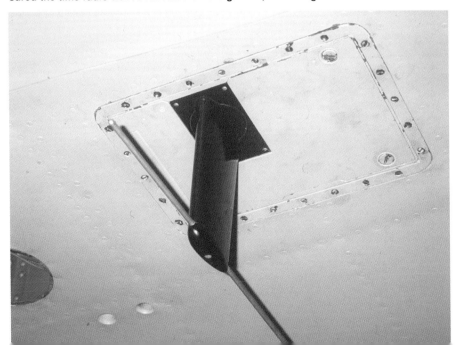

Navigation lights are located at each wingtip forward edge: red to port and green to starboard. The outer FuG 101a antenna stands out against the RLM04 Yellow (FS33538) wing tip undersurface. The leading edge slat is deployed in the extended position. This slat postponed airflow breakaway at high angles of attack to delay an aircraft's stall.

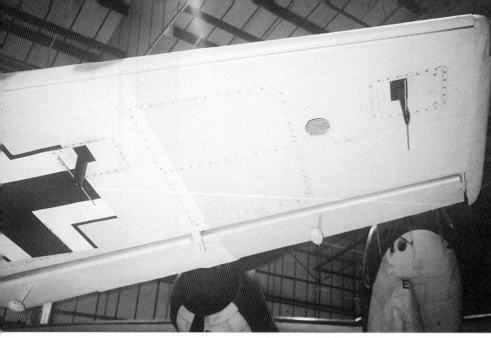

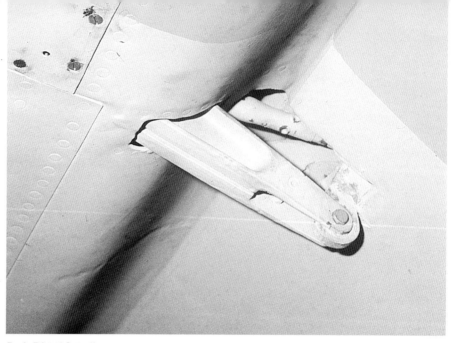

Twin mass balances are mounted under the port aileron; the starboard aileron was also fitted with these balances. The inner balance is positioned towards the aileron-end and the outer balance is between the aileron's center and outer edges. Mass balances reduce aileron flutter caused by airflow over the aileron's surface.

Late production Bf 110G-4s mounted the pitot tube on the starboard wingtip adjacent to the navigation light. Earlier Bf 110s placed this tube several feet in from the wingtip with its base slotting in under the wing leading edge. The pitot tube collected airflow to measure the aircraft's speed.

Both Bf 110G-4 ailerons are secured to the wing by three hinges. The hinges are located at the inboard and outboard ends and in the aileron's center. The circular hinge attachment is fitted to the inner face of the aileron slot. This hinge connects with the aileron actuator rod located above the bracket.

The Bf 110G-4's main landing light is located in the port wing leading edge, slightly outboard of the auxiliary fuel tank centerline. The landing light cover has been removed to expose the clear light bulb and its reflector.

The detached landing light cover is made from clear Plexiglas – tinted yellow with age – within a metal frame painted to match the surrounding airframe. The landing light was turned on to illuminate the airfield ahead of the pilot during landing and subsequent taxiing on the ground.

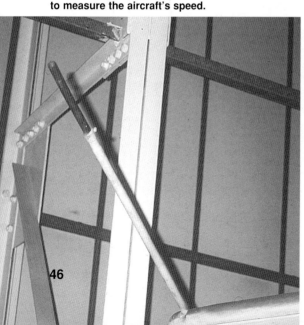

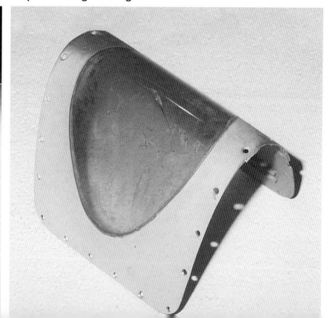

The Bf 110G-4's two coolant radiators are positioned outboard of the engines under the aft wing section. Air inlets into the radiator are braced in the center. The air passed through the radiator and carried away heat generated by the engine. The radiator's aft mounted flaps are offset towards the aircraft's wingtips.

Removal of the radiator fairing exposes the radiator's rectangular shape. Interior components were painted RLM02 Gray. Water and ethylene glycol in equal quantities form the coolant supply. This radiator is retained in place by attachments linked to both the engine cowling and the wing surface.

The radiator flap at the aft part of the radiator housing is open. When this flap is closed, it fits flush with a fairing mounted on the flap and extending to the flap trailing edge. The pilot could adjust the radiator flap to vary the cooling rate of the Bf 110G-4's two Daimler Benz DB 605B-1 engines.

The radiator fairing could be removed as a single unit. The radiator unit slots into the cover center-section when this fairing is installed on the aircraft. The radiator cover was secured to the Bf 110G-4's wing with flush fasteners.

The supercharger air intake for the Bf 110G-4's port engine is located in the wing leading edge. Air from the supercharger went to the engine's cylinders to increase power or to maintain power at high altitudes. One of the securing points for the auxiliary fuel tank sway braces is located at the front edge of the detachable wing panel.

The 78 gallon external fuel tank was secured to the wing through a mounting lug and strap at the tank's center. Fore-and-aft sway braces steadied the tank in flight, while two fuel leads ahead of the mount carried 87 octane aviation gasoline from the tank into the wing. The Bf 110D pioneered the carriage of external fuel tanks in the Bf 110 series.

The Bf 110G-4 could carry two 79 gallon (300 L) external fuel tanks under the wings for increased endurance. These fuel tanks composed the R7 modification (*Rüstsatz*; Field Conversion Set) available for the Bf 110G-2 through G-4 variants. Other *Rüstsätze* available for Bf 110Gs added different weapons to the aircraft.

The sway braces were anchored to the external fuel tank using threaded nuts. The fuel tank mounting lug slots into a separate aperture from those for the fuel leads. A trigger release lever for the tank is positioned at rear of main aperture; the tank can only be removed when the aircraft is on the ground.

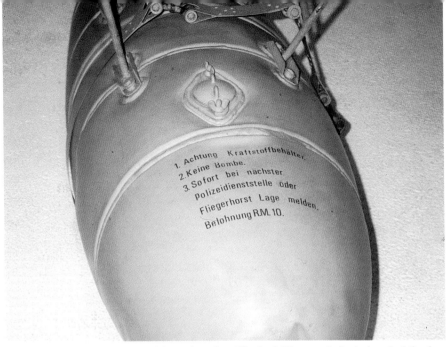

This external tank is detached from the wing. The fuel filler cap is just ahead of the forward sway braces and is held in place by butterfly nuts. Stenciling on the tank's nose warns anyone finding this item that it is a fuel tank, not a bomb, and to report this to the nearest Air Force or Police unit. A reward of 10 Reichmarks is also stated!

The port reserve fuel tank has been detached from the Bf 110G-4's wing. The 69 gallon (260.5 L) self-sealing tank is wrapped inside a protective rubberized cover. Fuel leaking out of a damaged tank contacts the rubber, which soon swells to block the hole and stop the leak.

Reserve fuel tank compartments are located behind the main spars and between the fuselage and the engine nacelles. The interior surfaces of the unpainted Alclad panels are stamped with a winged figure emblem. Cover panels are quickly detachable, which assists in the swift removal of the fuel tanks.

The reserve fuel tank is filled through the large circular aperture, positioned on the forward inside edge. The Bf 110G-4's pair of 69 gallon tanks and two 99 gallon (375 L) main tanks gave the aircraft a maximum internal fuel capacity of 336 gallons (1271 L).

49

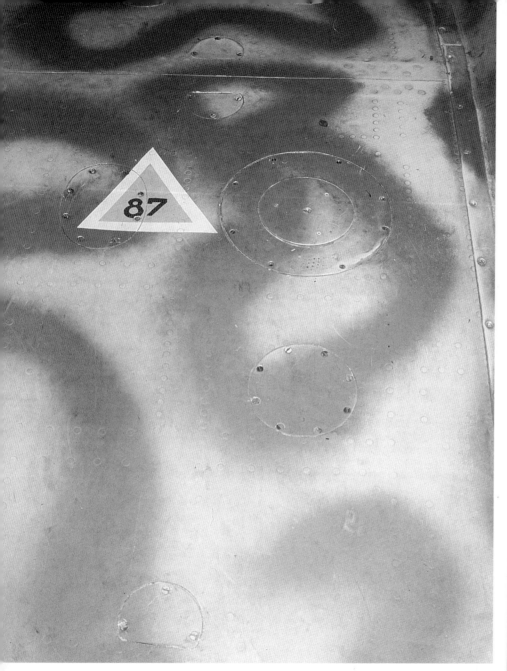

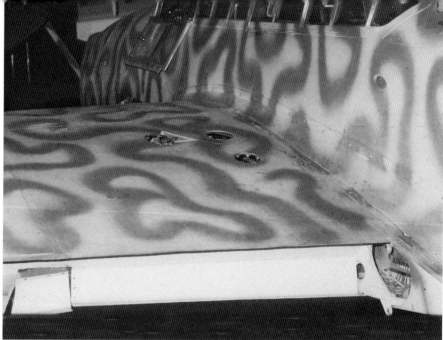

The access panels for the two port fuel tank filler caps and the fuel pumps are located on the Bf 110G-4's upper wing surface. The main tank filler cap is placed ahead of the auxiliary tank filler; the starboard wing tank arrangement is identical. The fuel tanks and flap are removed from this aircraft.

The dark brown and white triangle directly behind the engine oil tank cover bears the white word *Rotring* – the trade name of the oil used by this Luftwaffe aircraft. The Bf 110G-4's two engine oil tanks each held 9.3 gallons (35 L) of engine lubricant.

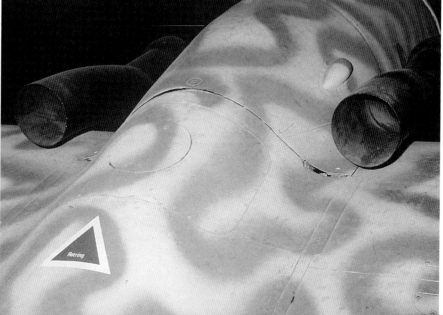

The port reserve fuel tank fill cover is placed on the aft upper wing alongside the wing-fuselage joint. The yellow and white triangle beside the filler cover alerts ground crewmen to fill the Bf 110's fuel tanks with 87 octane aviation gasoline. Other DB 605-powered Luftwaffe aircraft – including the Bf 109G – also used 87 octane fuel.

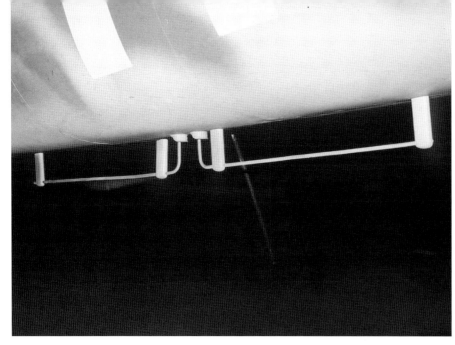

The Bf 110G-4's FuB (*Funk Blind*; Blind Landing Radio) 12F ILS (Instrument Landing System) employed twin ventral antennas for use in 'blind' landing conditions. The antennas are mounted along the aircraft centerline directly below the white outline *Balkenkreuz* (Balkan Cross) national marking.

Forward of the aircraft's jacking point – beside the code letter L – is the following: *Hier anheben Vor dem Aufbocken m.300kg belasten* (Weigh down the tail with 300 KG [660 lbs] prior to hoisting here). The number 14 above the aft FuB 12F antenna indicates one of the Bf 110G-4's 18 structural frames, numbered from front to rear.

The FuG 25a IFF (Identification Friend or Foe) antenna is mounted adjacent to the FuB 12F antennas and angled slightly aft from the rear fuselage. The IFF equipment sends a coded signal to inform German aircraft and ground stations of the Bf 110's friendly status.

The Bf 110G-4's downward identification light – missing its Plexiglas cover – is housed in a small fairing. This fairing is positioned ahead of the ILS (Instrument Landing System) antennas and slightly to port of the fuselage centerline. The white identification light signaled the aircraft's presence to German airfields and ground defenses.

Access to the rear fuselage radio equipment is through a square hatch on the port fuselage side, aft of the wing trailing edge. The access cover is manufactured from softwood or plywood – a late war substitute for increasingly scarce metal – and is secured by four corner screws. The FuG 10P's dynamo is placed on the lower equipment bay area.

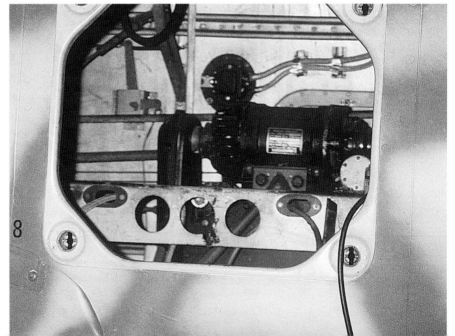

Along the starboard aft fuselage wall is the Siemens-Schuckert dynamo (generator) for the FuG (*Funk Geräte*; Radio Device) 10P HF (High Frequency) radio set. The dynamo and the radio equipment were accessed through a hatch mounted on the port fuselage side. The circular housing immediately below the FuG 10P is the filler point for the liquid oxygen bottles.

The shelf for the FuG 10P's dynamo is placed in the lower starboard area of the radio bay, aft of the rear cockpit. The large diagonal tube connects with the cockpit air vent on the starboard fuselage surface. This vent brings fresh air into the cockpits while the Bf 110 flies at low altitude.

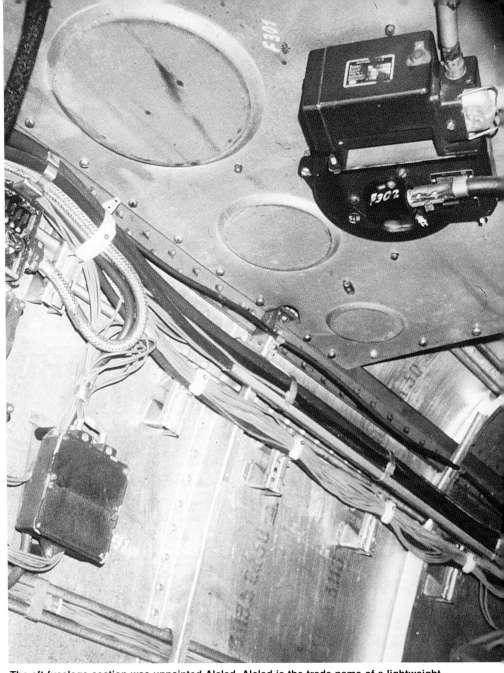

The aft fuselage section was unpainted Alclad. Alclad is the trade name of a lightweight, yet strong metal alloy coated with corrosion-resistant aluminum. Unpainted interior surfaces were a regular feature on late production Luftwaffe aircraft. Yellow electrical cables run along the inside of the aft fuselage, while the black box on the upper interior surface is believed to be associated with the Bf 110G-4's direction finding equipment.

(Above Left) This non-detachable panel aft of the rear cockpit enclosed the box structure containing the Bf 110G-4's *Anpeilungsgearet* (direction finding set). The Direction Finder (DF) receiver indicated the bearing of continuous wave signals sent by ground stations. The aircraft's pilot confirmed his flight path by tuning into the signals received by the DF device.

(Above) The open cockpit air vent is located on the starboard fuselage aft of the wing trailing edge. Immediately above this vent is the base for the auxiliary radio antenna wire, which connects with the main wire antenna running from the mast placed atop the canopy to the starboard vertical stabilizer. The blue and white cover aft of the air vent is the oxygen filler point. The black wording on this cover states: *Sauerstoff Öl u. Fettfrei halten* (Oxygen – keep free of oil and grease). Liquid oxygen used for breathing by the flight crew at high altitude is pumped through this filler point into the oxygen bottles placed inside the aft fuselage. The red and black cover below and forward of the oxygen filler vent cover denotes the 24 volt auxiliary starting connector, through which external electrical power was supplied to the aircraft while on the ground.

(Left) The main cockpit air vent cover is operated from the cockpit. The cover fits flush with the fuselage surface when the vent is closed. Fresh air from this vent is circulated throughout the fore and aft cockpits.

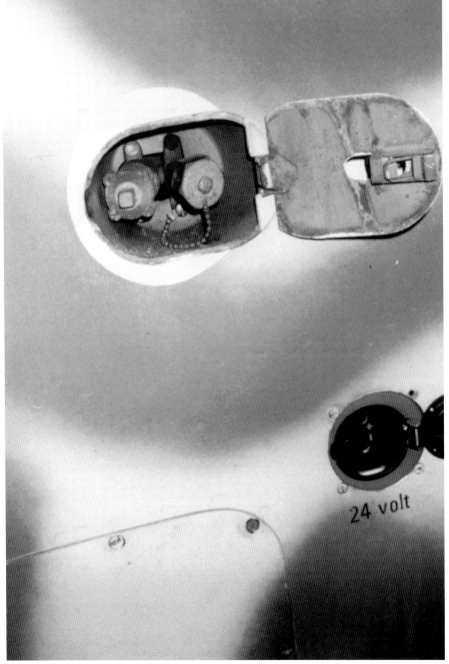

The flush fitting hatches for the oxygen fill point and the auxiliary starting connector open forward on single hinges. Caps cover the two liquid oxygen fill connections – one for each set of the Bf 110G-4's oxygen bottles. The black stencil *24 volt* beneath the auxiliary starter indicates the electrical power voltage used to operate aircraft systems on the ground.

The auxiliary antenna wire cover has been removed from its position directly above the cockpit air vent. Three small holes around the antenna wire base opening held flush fasteners used to secure the base cover in place. The antenna wire ran from the radio inside the fuselage, through a small hole in the cover, and then up to the main antenna wire running from the antenna mast to the aircraft's starboard vertical stabilizer.

The round-shaped master compass access panel is overpainted with the upper portion of the code letter R. This compass is positioned on cross supports in the upper half of the fuselage. The aircraft letter R beside the *Balkenkreuz* was incorrectly painted black by the museum. This letter was normally yellow or black with a yellow outline to indicate a 3. *Staffel* (squadron) aircraft.

The aft fuselage contained a reinforced section to jack up the tail. The black stencil *Hier aufbocken* (Jack up here) appears above and ahead of the tail wheel. Recommended tire pressure for the tailwheel (2.5 atmospheres) is stenciled above and aft of the strut. Twin fairing panels cover the stabilizer/fuselage junction.

The Bf 110G-4's aft fuselage gently narrows from the aft cockpit to the tail assembly. The aft fuselage surface is free of protrusions, apart from the open cabin air vent door aft of the rear cockpit. The RLM04 Yellow (FS33538) aft fuselage band appeared on all *Zerstöreren* (Destroyers) assigned to Reich Defense duties. The black fuselage code letters D5 and RL flank the white outline *Balkankreuz* (Balkan cross).

The Bf 110's tailwheel was originally intended to be retractable; however, this unit was subsequently fixed in position during prototype trials. The basic tailwheel design remained unchanged through the G model. The semi-gloss black wheel hub features a spoked pattern.

# Tailwheel and Strut Assembly

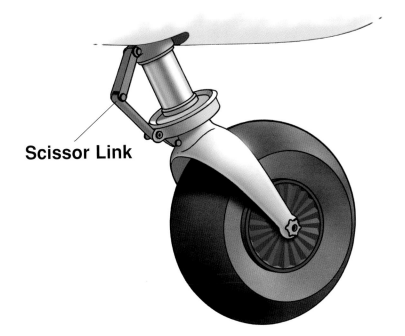

Scissor Link

The Bf 110's tailwheel is mounted into a VDM fork-shaped unit, which has a spring shock absorber and an oleo damper. The tire surface bears the standard lateral tread common to Luftwaffe aircraft. The RAF Museum placed the Bf 110G-4's tailwheel on parallel blocks to raise the tire off the floor and reduce pressure on the tailwheel unit.

# Tailwheel Strut Installation in Aft Fuselage

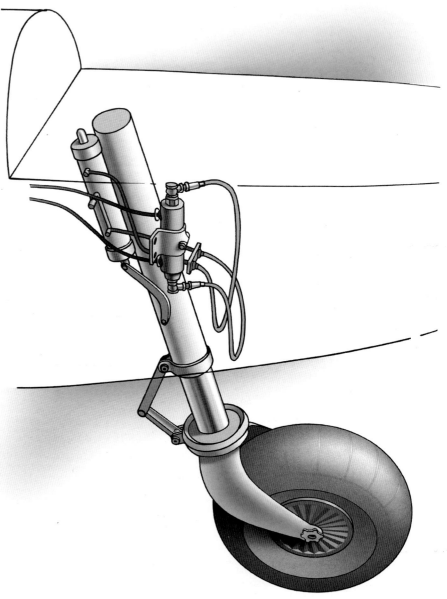

The Bf 110G-4's tailwheel yoke is angled forward at its base, then extends vertically into the fuselage. The Vee-shaped scissor link ahead of the yoke 'collar' prevents both wheel shimmy and over-extension of the chromed oleo strut inside the gear leg. The tailwheel strut is painted RLM76 Light Gray, while the wheel is semi-gloss black.

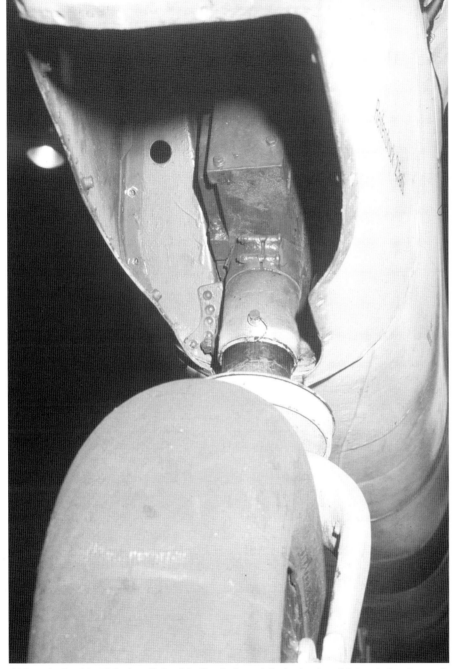

Although the Bf 110G-4's tailwheel is fixed, the original wheel well intended to house it when retracted has been left unfaired. The Bf 110V-1 prototype and Bf 110A series aircraft were equipped with a retracting tailwheel; however, this feature was dropped beginning with the Bf 110B. The tailwheel swivels through 360° while the Bf 110 maneuvers on the ground.

The tailwheel strut yoke is slotted into the base of a block-pattern mounting at the wheel well's front. Mounted on the starboard side of this well is the elevator operating mechanism rod. Aircraft restorers painted this Bf 110's wheel well interior red primer; the Germans usually painted this area RLM02 Gray (FS36165). The tailwheel well was normally sealed with a canvas cover fastened to the studs surrounding the opening.

Three formed metal strips covered the vertical stabilizer's leading edge. Each strip is secured in place by two screws. The *Hakenkreuz* (hooked cross, or swastika) – the Nazi party emblem – appeared on the tails of Luftwaffe aircraft from 1935 until the end of World War II ten years later. This white edged black swastika on this Bf 110G was one variation of this emblem painted on Luftwaffe aircraft.

Flexible radio antenna cable lead attachments are located on top of each vertical stabilizer. These attachments are connected to small pulleys inside the fin and function as inertia reels for the antennas. This arrangement keeps the antennas steady, particularly when the Bf 110G-4 is in flight.

The Bf 110G-4 introduced a larger rudder than those of earlier Bf 110s, a feature which improved the aircraft's handling. The vertical tail surfaces are finished in the distinctive *Wellenmuster* (wave pattern) camouflage scheme of RLM75 Gray Violet (FS36122) waves over RLM76 Light Gray (FS36473). The aircraft's *Werke Nummer* (factory number) 730301 is black on the upper vertical stabilizer surface.

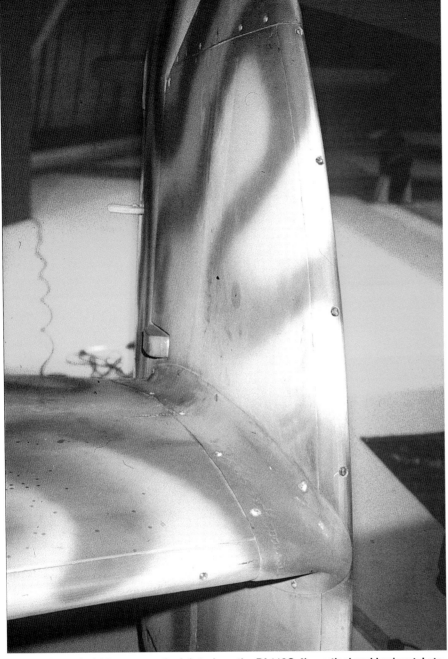

An aerodynamic fairing covers the joint where the Bf 110G-4's vertical and horizontal stabilizers meet. Strips covering the leading edges were installed using flush fitting screws. The Bf 110's tail, in common with the rest of the aircraft, used an all-metal structure covered by an aluminum alloy skin. The protrusion along the aft section of the vertical stabilizer is a rudder trim tab actuator fairing.

The fin/rudder joint runs vertically except at the top of the vertical stabilizer, where the joint angles forward to function as an aerodynamic balance. The rudder is attached in the center by a large hinge. Two smaller hinges were located at the top and bottom. The Bf 110G larger rudder replaced the rounded-edge design employed by earlier Bf 110 variants. The newer Bf 110G-4 also used a larger rudder trim tab than earlier aircraft.

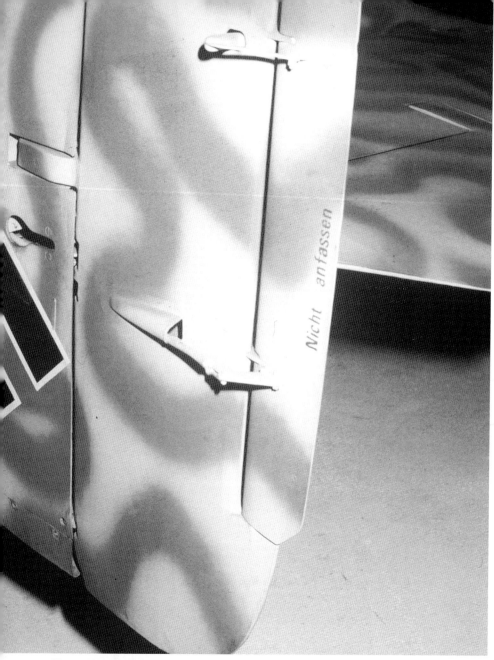

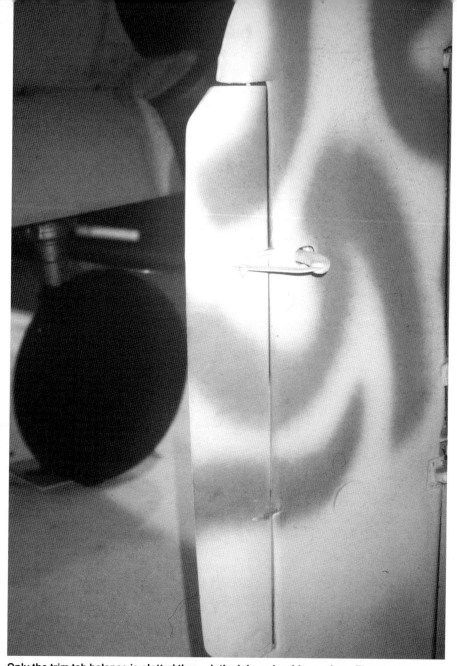

The rudder trim tab is mounted to the rudder by the lower hinge-and-rod coupling feeding into a fairing. The upper hinge serves as the trim tab balance. The Bf 110G's trim tab extends beyond the rudder's trailing edge; earlier Bf 110 models featured trim tabs flush with the rudder's trailing edge. The red lettering on the tab reads *Nicht anfassen* (Do not touch).

Only the trim tab balance is slotted through the inboard rudder surface. The trim tab hinge does not have a rod coupling on this surface. The pilot operates the trim tabs using a lever positioned on the starboard cockpit console. Trim tabs reduced the loads on the control surfaces, making the aircraft easier to fly.

The Bf 110's elevators – like the rudders and ailerons – are made of metal frames covered with fabric. A trim tab was fitted to each elevator. The elevators' outer edges are angled back and inwards to permit full lateral movement for the rudders.

## Bf 110G Vertical Stabilizer

The port rudder has been turned to its maximum angle of operation for a left turn. Maximum rudder application was extremely difficult to achieve in practice, given the air pressure working against its movement. Both Bf 110 rudders move in unison to provide the aircraft with yaw (side-to-side) control.

63

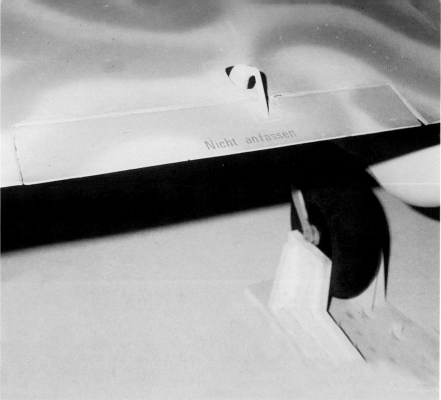

(Above Left) The Bf 110G-4's starboard elevator is positioned in a maximum degree of depression for diving. This extreme use of the elevators would never be deployed in flight, due to the air pressure acting upon these control surfaces. Both elevators operate in unison to provide the Bf 110G-4 with pitch (up-and-down) control. The trim tab mounted on the elevator's trailing edge is deployed in an upward counter-position.

(Above) A trim tab incorporates a balance. The red stenciling *Nicht anfassen* (Do not touch) is applied to all three sets of the Bf 110G-4's trim tabs – elevators, rudders, and ailerons – to warn the aircraft's ground crewmen. These tabs could be damaged if improperly treated by maintenance personnel.

(Left) The elevator trim tab actuating rod is placed inboard of the trim tab balance on the elevator's undersurface. This actuating rod enters the elevator fabric forward of the balance and is operated by the elevator trim tab wheel, located in the port forward cockpit wall. Bf 110 trim tabs are metal, while the aircraft's control surfaces are fabric-covered.

64

The pilot could increase the stabilizer's angle of incidence up to 4° above the aircraft's centerline using a handwheel in the cockpit. A jack mounted inside the tail raised or lowered the horizontal stabilizer as required to alter the Bf 110G-4's handling. The rectangular outline at the front center stabilizer area is the 'break-point' where the stabilizer meets the aft fuselage.

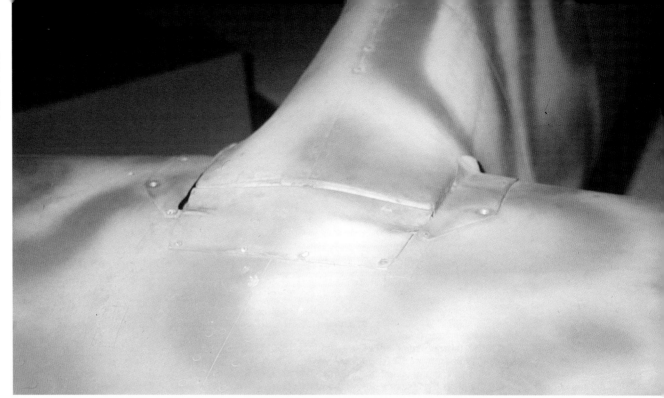

Three light sockets are mounted on the aft end of the Bf 110G-4's tail cone, parallel with the trailing edges of the elevators. The center socket held the white identification light, while the red navigation light would be installed in the port socket and the green light in the starboard socket. All three light bulbs have been removed from this Bf 110G-4.

Snow coats this Bf 110G-2 (*Werke Nummer*/Factory Number 120037) assigned to the *Dackelstaffel* (Dachshund Squadron) of JG (*Jagdgeschwader*; Fighter Wing) 5. The first Bf 110Gs were delivered to this Norway-based unit during early 1943. The 1B code letters on this aircraft replaced the original LN codes during the latter stages of World War II.

An airman rests beneath the port engine nacelle of a early Bf 110G-2. This original G model included vertical access panels for the four nose-mounted 7.92MM MG17 machine gun ammunition containers. The sealed nose machine gun muzzle openings indicate the weapons have been removed from the nose of this aircraft.

Ground crewmen fill the port 79 gallon (300 L) auxiliary fuel tank on a Bf 110G-2 assigned to 13(Z)/JG 5 – a *Zerstörer* (Destroyer) squadron assigned to a day fighter wing. This aircraft's fuel tank is fitted to a different style of rack than was normally used with these tanks. A sand filter normally associated with desert operations is fitted to the carburetor intake and ETC 50 bomb racks are installed on the wing.

The dangerous proximity of a Bf 110G-2's spinning propeller is not inhibiting the horse-play of these II. *Gruppe* (Group)/ZG 76 personnel during the winter of 1943-44. The upper nose armament panel and weapons have been removed from the aircraft. Two 8.3 inch (21 CM) rocket tubes are mounted under the wing. The *Gruppe* was defending Germany against the daylight bombing raids of the 8th US Army Air Force.

Bf 110s were effective against unescorted bombers; however, the *Zerstöreren's* extreme vulnerability to Allied fighter escorts merited fighter cover by Fw 190s or Bf 109s. A *Rotte* (pair) of Bf 110G-2s perform a line-abreast take off with a Rotte of Fw 190s.

This 5/ZG 76 (*Zerstörergeschwader*; Destroyer Wing) Bf 110G-2 is equipped with the ventral pack containing a pair of 20MM MG 151/20 cannon. The nose armament consists of two 30MM Mk 108 cannon in the upper nose section and two further MG 151/20 cannon in the lower nose compartment. Flash eliminators were fitted to the muzzles of the 30MM Mk 108 weapons. Two 79 gallon external fuel tanks are carried under the wings.

A single 8.3 inch (21 CM) W.Gr (*Werfer Granate*; Mortar Shell) 21 rocket tube has been installed on this Bf 110G-2; normally, two W.Gr. 21 tubes were mounted under each outer wing. The ventral mounted 20MM MG 151/20 cannon's cover appears to have been removed, suggesting this aircraft is not about to take off on a mission.

A *Schwarm* (four-ship formation) of Bf 110G-2s fly low over the snow-covered German countryside and are probably returning from a mission. The fighters belong to II/ZG 76, which completed nearly one year of *Reichsverteidigung* (Reich Defense) duties in the fall of 1944. The Geschwader then exchanged its Bf 110s for Bf 109s and was redesignated JG 76.

A Luftwaffe engine oil tank trailer is displayed next to the RAF Museum's Bf 110G-4. Ground crewmen used this trailer to fill the Bf 110's engine oil tanks, using the hose placed on top of the tank. Three braces – including one obscured by the starboard wheel – maintain the trailer's upright position when it is removed from the towing vehicle. The oil tank trailer's color does not appear to equate to a specific RLM (*Reichsluftfahrtministerium*; Reich Air Ministry) paint category, but is believed to be a mix of RLM75 Gray Violet and RLM76 Light Gray.

# Bf 110G Upper Surface Color Schemes

## Day Fighter

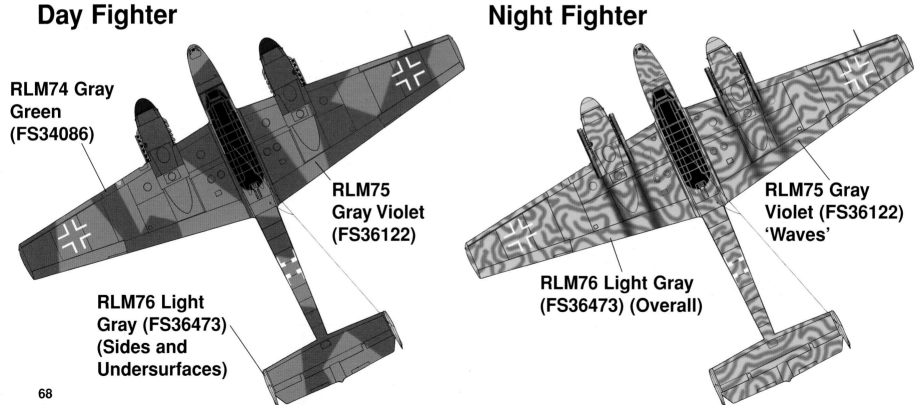

RLM74 Gray Green (FS34086)

RLM75 Gray Violet (FS36122)

RLM76 Light Gray (FS36473) (Sides and Undersurfaces)

## Night Fighter

RLM75 Gray Violet (FS36122) 'Waves'

RLM76 Light Gray (FS36473) (Overall)

A Luftwaffe flight crew mannequin is posed beside the RAF Museum's Bf 110G-4. This figure is wearing the light tan *Kombination* (flight suit) equipped with zip pockets on the sides and above the knees. The light tan flying helmet is fitted with black built-in earphone covers and is accompanied by goggles. The yellow life preserver was inflated to keep the airman's head above water in the event of a ditching. The fur-lined flight boots are fitted with top mounted retaining straps and side zippers.

The second figure posed by the RAF Museum's Bf 110G-4 represents a *Luftwaffe-Hilferin* – a female auxiliary employed on administrative support duties. Her simple gray uniform – forage cap, jacket, and skirt – is completed with black shoes and necktie and a white shirt. The teletype operator insignia is worn on the left jacket sleeve. The clothing material's basic quality is typical of the German uniforms produced towards the end of World War II.

A II. *Gruppe* (Group)/ZG (*Zerstörergeschwader*; Destroyer Wing) 1 Bf 110G-2 flies past Mount Vesuvius in southern Italy. The Wing regularly displayed the *Wespe* (Wasp) design on the noses of their Bf 110s. II/ZG 1 was stationed in Italy from 1942 until the early summer of 1943, when the Gruppe was transferred back to Germany for Reich Defense duties.

Two Bf 110G-2 are prepared for a night fighter mission while assigned to NJG (*Nachtjagdgeschwader*; Night Fighter Wing) 200. This Geschwader served primarily on the Eastern Front and used *Helle Nachtjagd* (Illuminated Night Fighter) tactics to combat the scattered and small scale nature of Red (Soviet) Air Force incursions. These Soviet raids were often conducted at medium or low levels, where ground-control guidance proved relatively difficult compared to conditions in Western Europe.

Two Bf 110G-2s assigned to 13.(Z)/JG (*Jagdgeschwader*; Fighter Wing) 5 fly over northern Norway's barren landscape during 1943 or 1944. This *Zerstörer* (Destroyer) unit was nick-named the *Dackelstaffel* (Dachshund Squadron; more specifically, Badger-dog Squadron). Both fighters carry 79 gallon (300 L) external fuel tanks under the wings. JG 5 operated over Norway, Finland, and the northwestern Soviet Union during this period of World War II.

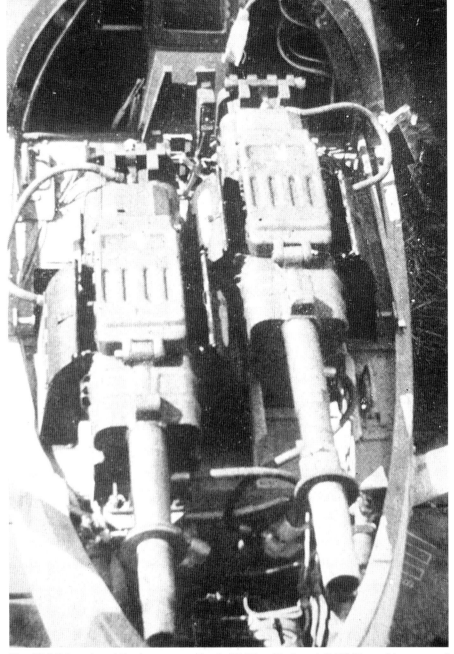

The Bf 110G replaced the four nose-mounted 7.92ᴍᴍ Rheinmetall MG17 machine guns of earlier variants with two 30ᴍᴍ Rheinmetall Mk 108 cannons. The Mk 108 used the blow-back operating system, which reloaded the next ammunition cartridge by blowing back the previous cartridge case from the breech mechanism. The brilliant muzzle flash tended to blind the pilot and was an unfavorable aspect of this weapon.

A Rb (*Reihenbildkammer*; aerial mapping camera) 50/30 film canister is placed into a Bf 110G-3's aft cockpit, where the camera will be positioned on the center of the floor. The Bf 110G-3 reconnaissance variant deleted the ventral armament to allow operating room for the camera. The Bf 110G series introduced the side-hinged aft cockpit entry hatch. The airman standing on the wing wears a combination of overalls and a leather *Fliegerjacke* (flying jacket).

13.(Z)/JG (*Jagdgeschwader*; Fighter Wing) 5 operated the Messerschmitt Bf 110G-2 between early 1943 and the unit's dissolution in the final months of World War II. The *Zerstörer* (Destroyer) Squadron to which 1B+LX was assigned operated with the rest of the Wing in Norway.

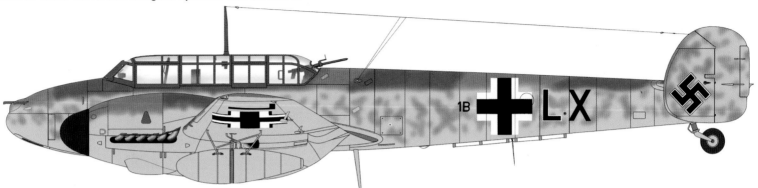

This Bf 110G-2/R3 (DT+MR) was assigned to *Blindflugschule* (Blind Flying School) B 38 at Seerappen during late 1943 and 1944. RLM04 Yellow (FS33538) aft fuselage bands denote the unit's specialist function – training pilots to operate under Instrument Flight Rules (IFR).

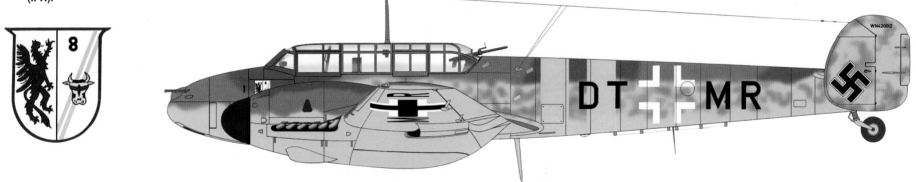

This Bf 110G-2 was assigned to II/ZG (*Zerstörergeschwader*; Destroyer Wing) 1 when the *Gruppe* (Group) was serving in Italy during late 1943. Allied forces found this aircraft (S9+FM) abandoned on Montecorvino airfield, near the Salerno beachhead. ZG 1's *Wespe* (Wasp) emblem was painted on the noses of their Bf 110s.

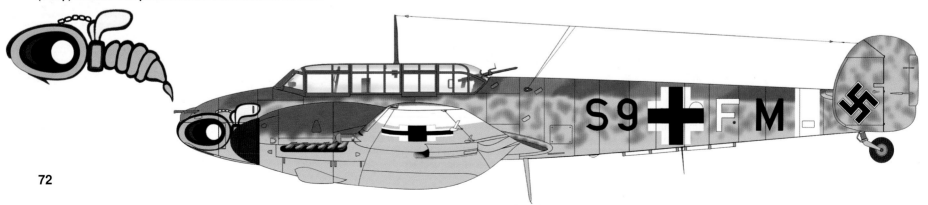

II/ZG 76 operated the Bf 110G-2 on *Reichsverteidigung* (Defense of the Reich) duties over Germany during 1943 and 1944. This aircraft (2N+AM) belongs to the *Geschwader's* 4th *Staffel* (Squadron).

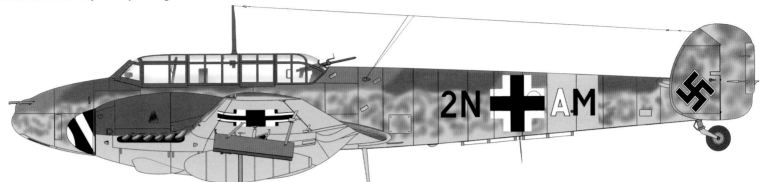

This Bf 110G-4 (3C+BR) was operated by 7/NJG (*Nachtjagdgeschwader*; Night Fighter Wing) 4 during 1943-1944. The Wing converted to the Junkers Ju 88G towards the end of 1944. Some Luftwaffe night fighters had black starboard wing undersurfaces to provide instant identification for German anti-aircraft gunners.

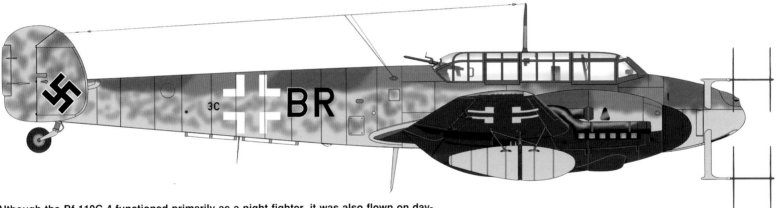

Although the Bf 110G-4 functioned primarily as a night fighter, it was also flown on daylight sorties against USAAF heavy bombers through early 1944. This particular aircraft (D5+LT) was assigned to 9./NJG 3.

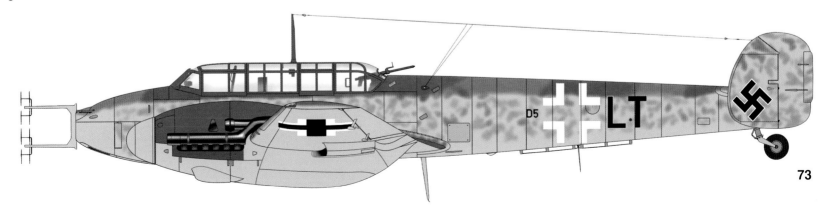

(Below) This Bf 110G-4 (3C+BT) of III/NJG 4 is equipped with the FuG 202 (*Lichtenstein* BC) radar – the first airborne interception radar carried by Luftwaffe night fighters. The FuG 202 entered operational service in February of 1942. The four nose-mounted 7.92MM MG17 machine guns are augmented by the ventral-mounted pair of 20mm MG151/20 cannon. This Bf 110G-4 was based at Juvincourt/Reims, France during early 1944.

(Above) This 6./NJG 6 Bf 110G-4 (2Z+OP, *Werke Nummer* 5547) landed in Dübendorf, Switzerland due to a 'navigation error' on 15 March 1944. A FuG 202 (*Lichtenstein* BC) radar is mounted in the nose. The aircraft is primarily finished in RLM76 Light Gray with bands of RLM74 Gray Green and RLM75 Gray Violet along the fuselage. The starboard wing undersurface and external fuel tank are black. The propeller blades and spinners are RLM70 Black Green. The MG81Z machine gun has been removed from the rear cockpit.

(Below) These two Bf 110G-4/R3 night fighters assigned to 7./NJG 4 have nose-mounted antennas for the FuG 220 (Model B) radar. The FuG 220's improved minimum-range capability dispensed with the need for the earlier FuG 212, which had previously provided this vital aspect of interception. These aircraft have black starboard wing undersurfaces as a 'friendly' recognition guide to German anti-aircraft batteries.

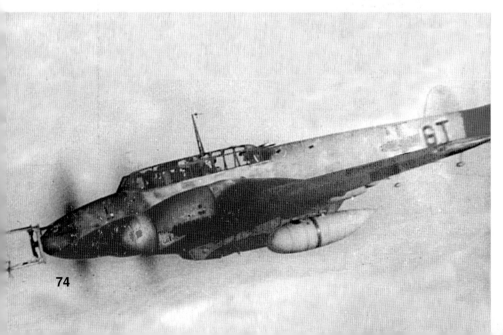

The twin 20MM Oerlikon MGFF/M cannon comprising the *schräge Musik* (slanting, or jazz music) installation appears through a Bf 110G-4's silhouetted canopy. The upward-firing cannon were set at 60 to 70˚ angles to fire upward into a bomber's undersurfaces. The 7.92MM MG81Z rear machine gun is installed for the rear gunner's use against enemy aircraft, such as Mosquito escort fighters.

This BF 110G-4's *schräge Musik* layout displays two variations to the normal installation. The two 20MM MGFF/M cannon are replaced by two 30MM Mk 108 cannon, while the guns are aligned fore-and-aft instead of the normal lateral arrangement. Approximately 50 percent of all German night fighter attacks used these upward-firing weapons during the last two years of World War II.

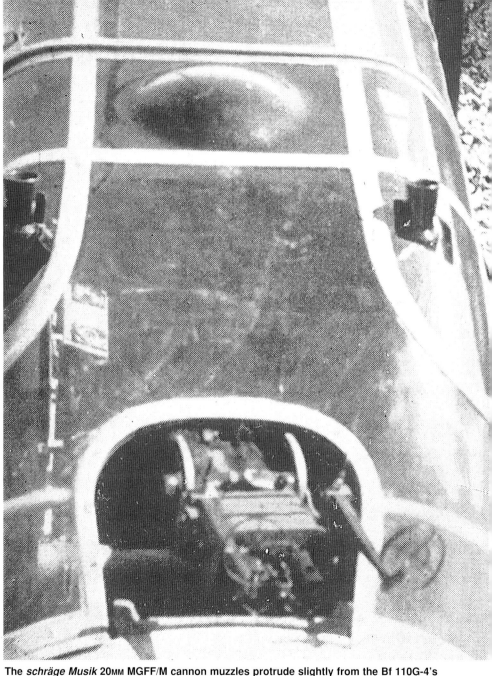

The *schräge Musik* 20MM MGFF/M cannon muzzles protrude slightly from the Bf 110G-4's rear canopy. Conical flash hiders on the muzzles reduced the blinding flash from the weapon's fire from being seen by the rear cockpit crewmen. The 7.92MM MG81Z machine gun was equipped with a ring-and-bead gunsight, in which the gunner aimed the post near the breech at the center of the ring near the muzzle.

The pilot of this 6/NJG 6 Bf 110G-4/R1 (2Z+OP, Werke Nummer 5547), due to a navigation error, landed in Dübendorf, Switzerland on 15 March 1944. This navigation error was a feint, because the Swiss later returned the aircraft to the Luftwaffe. The pilot was granted political asylum.

*Hauptmann* (Captain) Wilhelm Johnen of 5/NJG 5 force-landed this Bf 110G-4/R3 (C9+EN) in Dübendorf, Switzerland on 28 April 1944. The Swiss destroyed the fighter in agreement with the Germans, who wished to prevent the secrets of the Bf 110G-4's FuG 212 and FuG 220 radars from falling into Allied hands.

This Bf 110G-4 (3C+LB) belongs to *Stab* (Headquarters) I/NJG 4. It bears a distinctive sharkmouth design on the nose, which was originally used by the Bf 110s of II/ZG 76, the *Haifischgruppe* (Shark Group).

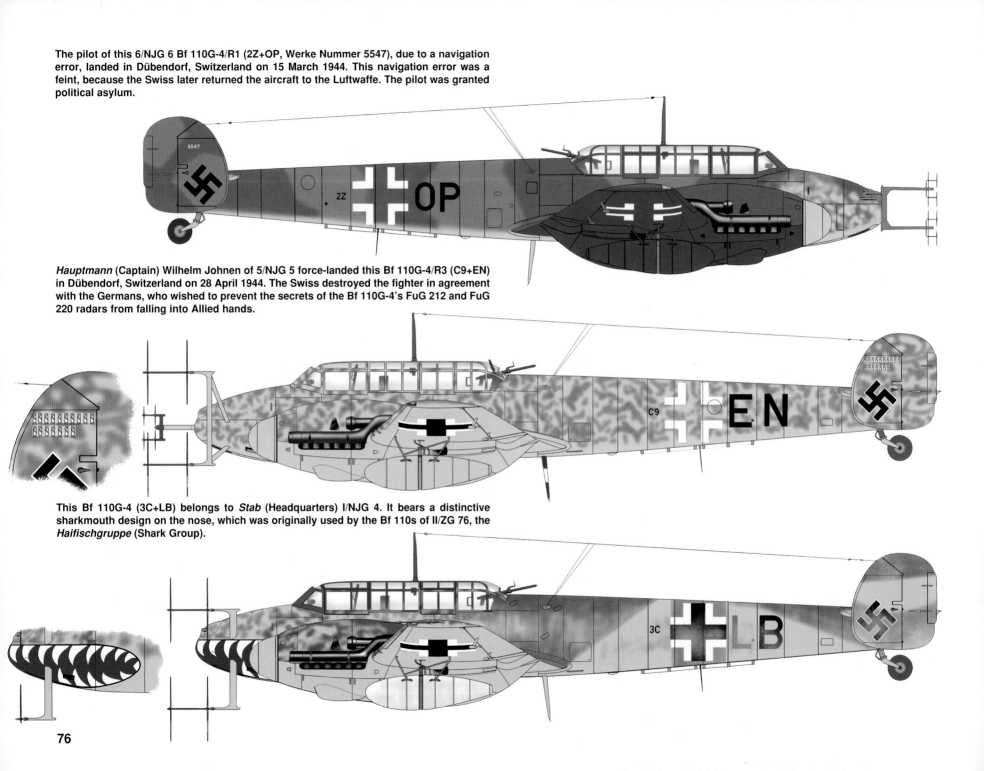

NJG 1 operated the Bf 110 throughout World War II, although the Wing was almost wholly converted to the Ju 88 by 1945. This 9/NJG1 aircraft (G9+HT, W.Nr. 160128) was based at Fritzer, Germany in April of 1945.

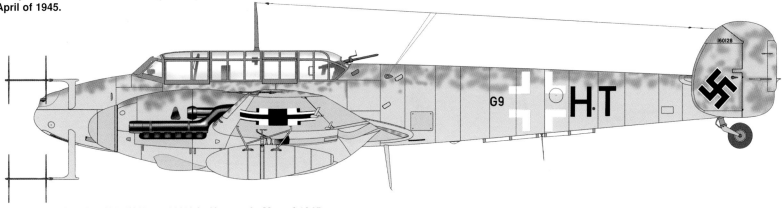

British units discovered this Bf 110G-4 (B4+KA, W.Nr. 110087) in Norway in May of 1945. The fighter carries code letters for a *Geschwader Stab* (Wing Headquarters) aircraft; however, the unit to which this aircraft belongs is recorded as a single night fighter *Staffel*. The unit first operated in Finland, then transferred to Norway in mid-1944.

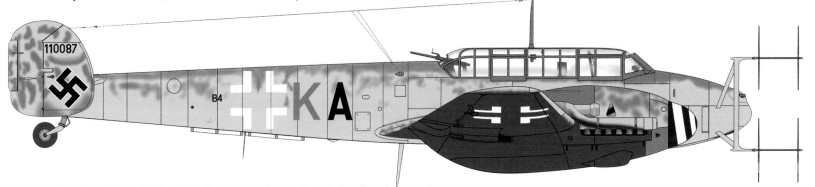

This Bf 110G-4 night fighter (W.Nr. 160750) was one of many found abandoned on an airfield at Brunswick, Germany in 1945. The aircraft wears the late war night fighter camouflage scheme of RLM75 over RLM76, with black outline fuselage crosses.

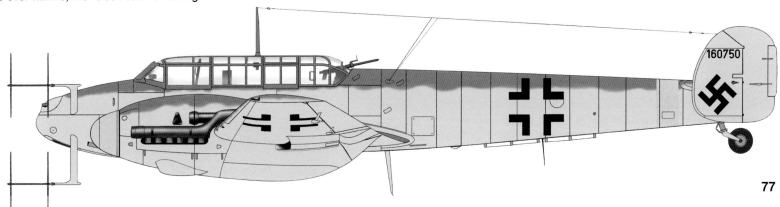

*Major* Willi Hergt is strapped into the pilot's seat while his two crewmates complete final preparations for an operational sortie. Hergt assumed command of I/NJG 4 in mid-1942, becoming an *Experte* (Expert) with 73 *Abschuße* ('kills') by war's end. His final assignment was flying the Me 262 jet fighter with JV (*Jagdverband*; Fighter Formation) 44.

This Bf 110G-4 (W.Nr. 160750) is parked at Bad Kösen airfield, Germany in June of 1945. The aircraft bears the final Luftwaffe night fighter camouflage scheme of RLM75 Gray Violet uppersurfaces over RLM76 Light Gray undersurfaces. The rear fuselage band is RLM04 Yellow. The Bf 110G-4's radar antenna masts are the simplified 'X' design associated with the FuG 220 Model D radar.

A Luftwaffe technician examines this Bf 110G-4's radar antennas. The central antenna belongs to the FuG 212 radar, whose minimum-range capability was vastly superior to the early FuG 220 set with which it was linked. The FuG 212 was deleted when later FuG 220 variants with enhanced minimum-range capability were installed on Luftwaffe night fighters. FuG 220 antenna support frames were also simplified to an 'X-shaped' design.

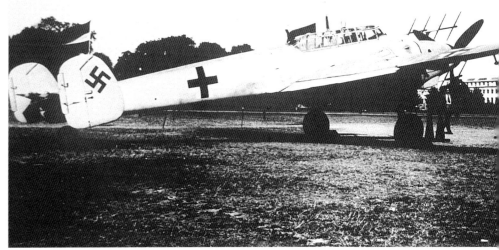

Allied soldiers inspect the broken airframe of a Bf 110G night fighter abandoned at Brunswick-Waggum, Germany after the end of World War II. This aircraft is painted in the late night fighter camouflage scheme of RLM75 over RLM76. Balkankreuz national markings are simple black or white outlines. The fuselage outline crosses were white until the final camouflage scheme was introduced in early 1945.

The captured Bf 110G-4 displayed in London is equipped with FuG 220 air intercept radar. The FuG 220 antennas are angled at 45° to combat the worst effects of RAF radar countermeasures. The electronic war pitting German radars against British countermeasures lasted throughout World War II. The engine exhausts are fitted with the Eberspacher straight pipe flame dampers installed on late war Bf 110G-4s.

This Bf 110G-4 shown in London was one of numerous Luftwaffe aircraft placed on public display following the end of World War II. The aircraft is fitted with the enlarged rudders, which were introduced on the Bf 110G to improve handling. The night fighter does not appear to be equipped with *schräge Musik* upward-firing guns.

The Royal Aircraft Establishment (RAE) at Farnborough, England evaluated a comprehensive range of Luftwaffe designs during 1945 and 1946. The German national markings on this Bf 110G-4 (W.Nr. 730037) have been replaced by British roundels on the wings and fuselage, with a fin flash placed on the vertical stabilizers. This and other captured aircraft were publicly displayed at Farnborough in the fall of 1945.

# More Luftwaffe Warplanes

**1030 Bf 110 Zerstörer**

**1044 Bf 109 Part 1**

**1057 Bf 109 Part 2**

**1073 Ju 87 Stuka**

**1170 Fw 190**

**5510 Fw 190D Walk Around**

**5522 Fw 190A/F Walk Around**

# from squadron/signal publications